With Water and Spirit

History of African American Apostolic Denominations In the U.S.

James C. Richardson

With Water and Spirit
James C. Richardson

ISBN: 978-1-938373-51-0
LCCN: 2020943622

Seymour Press
Capitol Heights, MD

WITH WATER AND SPIRIT

TABLE OF CONTENTS

ACKNOWLEDGMENTS

Much of this book was originally done as a Master of Divinity thesis at Howard University Divinity School. In this regard, I express profound gratitude to Dr. James D. Tyms, the faculty advisor. His critical reading of this manuscript and insightful wisdom have provided the writer so much help. My appreciation extends also to Dr. Leon E. Wright, the-co-faculty advisor. His depth and knowledge of the 'Pentecostal-Apostolic experience guided the author in the initial formulation of this thesis. I offer an abundance of thanks to Dr. Samuel L. Gandy, former dean of the Divinity School, the administration, faculty, and library staff. Had not the various support, knowledge, and able assistance been provided by these persons this book would have been severely impeded. A special thanks goes to Carole Staton for her many helpful suggestions. The writer is truly grateful to Roxie Ann Hairston for typing much of the manuscript.

I am also highly appreciative to the many people affiliated with the Black Apostolic Church. The request for interviews and the response shown for the need of various literature have been very gratifying. And while my gratitude extends to all the members of the Apostolic church, I especially thank my father, Bishop James C. Richardson, Sr., Bishop Morris E. Golder, Bishop Monroe R. Saunders, Sr., and Bishop Smallwood E. Williams. The wealth of information and life experiences shared with the author by these men will continue to be helpful in future years.

A special thanks goes to my wife, Gloria, and friends for technical assistance. Finally, I express gratitude to Dr. James S. Tinney, my publisher-editor for providing immeasurable editorial assistance.

WITH WATER AND SPIRIT

FOREWORD

Too often the Black Pentecostals have either been completely overlooked or woefully neglected in the writings of white Pentecostal historians; and it is because of this tremendous oversight that in recent years Black Pentecostals, eager to know their "roots and heritage," have engaged in serious research in order to leave our posterity some accounts of how Black Pentecostals came into existence. As it was with the "Jew-Gentile conflict" in the church of the first century; so, it has been with' 'the White-Black conflict" in the modern Pentecostal movement. It is true that St. Paul said that "there is no difference between the Jew and the Greek ... but all one in Christ Jesus" (Rom. 10:12; Gal. 3:28); but as the Gospel has met many culture patterns and societal mores, men have allowed their varying systems to override the "one body concept" (Eph. 4:4) of the church. It has been divided into the "white" and the "black" Pentecostal church. And such men as James Richardson have striven through diligent research to put the Black element of Pentecostalism in its proper perspective. It is the author's hope that this endeavor will give to the reader a greater knowledge of the total Pentecostal Church in the twentieth century.

Bishop Morris E. Golder, D.D.

PREFACE

In this age of Black consciousness and Black awareness, one fact that many have come to realize is this: the church in the Black community has always been the one institution its residents have controlled. Under the heading, "Black Church - Black Religion" one can find various groups that have developed. What are called mainline groups, such as Methodist and Baptist are here. Groups that are referred to as cults are prevalent. These include Daddy Grace's organization and the Peace Movement started by Father Divine. A third grouping of Black churches comes under the Pentecostal banner. One of the church movements that has experienced consistent growth since 1900 are the Black Pentecostal-Apostolic churches.

In this book, the author is using Black to designate those Apostolic denominations whose members are predominantly Afro-American or Bilalian.

These Black churches are described as Pentecostal because the members ascribe to and believe in the charismatic experience of speaking in tongues. Since it is taught that every believer must speak in tongues at least once, it is considered a normative Christian experience.

Going a step further, these Pentecostal churches are called Apostolic for two reasons. First, it is believed that water baptism must be administered "in the name of Jesus Christ," not in the Trinitarian formula. For the devotees, this church espouses a doctrine which refutes a belief in the doctrine of Trinity. Secondly, the members of this church believe that Jesus is God. In other words, Jehovah-God of the Old Testament is Jesus Christ-God of the New Testament.

Baptism in Jesus' name, receiving the Holy Ghost with the initial evidence of speaking in tongues, and the belief that Jesus is God, make up the foundation of the doctrine. These doctrinal points comprise the strand of commonality and unity in all Apostolic church organizations. If these points are characteristic, then just as characteristic of this church is a "split syndrome," a tendency to divide and form a new church. The author's list of splits, schisms and subsequent splinter groups that have occurred since 1919 in incomplete. Suffice it to say that if the splintering trend continues unabated, one wonders how effective the various Apostolic organizations will be relative to ministering in these times.

The purpose of this book is to show how the Black Apostolic church originated. The author contends that the theology of John Wesley has been very prominent in the development of this church. Therefore, in Chapter I, focusing on Wesley's doctrine of Sanctification, the author attempts to trace its influence. Starting with John Wesley in England and coming to America with the Methodists, the author then highlights the Holiness Movement. After emphasizing the contemporary Pentecostal movement, the birth of the Apostolic denominations is presented. The words organization and denomination are used synonymously.

The purpose also is to validate the author's claim that enough splits have occurred to indicate a negative syndrome. This is done in Chapter II by focusing on several Apostolic organizations. Practically all new Apostolic organizations come into being by separating from a previously existing group. The competitive infighting resulting from this pattern can only be self-defeating.

Because the thrust of this book is descriptive as well as historical, Chapter III deals with doctrine. The purpose is to present some of the beliefs, and thus, more understanding of the movement.

After presenting history, doctrine and information on a number of splits, the author offers some observations and suggestions. The purpose in this regard is to present some options and alternatives to the present predicament of Black Apostolic churches. This is done in the conclusion.

Finally, it is hoped that this book will serve to add to the scarce and limited written material on Black Apostolic churches.

Because the thrust is historical and descriptive, there is only minimal interpretative information. Additionally, all of the Apostolic organizations are not listed primarily for two reasons. First, the writer's knowledge of all the organizations is incomplete. He learns of other groups being formed almost every year. Secondly, the time that would be needed for travel and research to list all of the Black Apostolic organizations is not available.

Three methods have been used in the collection of data for this book. First was the historical approach. This consisted of library research and the use of various organizational literature. Secondly, persons have been encountered and data received by interviews. Thirdly, as a result of being reared in the Black Apostolic church, the author has also relied on personal experience.

.

WITH WATER AND SPIRIT

CHAPTER I

HISTORICAL BACKGROUND

If one looks at the brief historical sections of the discipline books of many of the Apostolic organizations, he will become aware of an interesting point. They all consider themselves to be a continuation of the great revival that began at Jerusalem on the Day of Pentecost, A.D. 33, as recorded in the second chapter of the Book of Acts.

In some instances, the writers or the editors of the hooks of these various organizations make passing reference to Tertullian, Chrysostom, the Quakers, and Wesley as connecting points from the first century to the twentieth century. Then the Apostolic groups inform us of the great revival that commenced in the state of Kansas in 1901 and moved Southward to Texas. For all practical purposes, this fact refers to Charles F. Parham and his contingent of Pentecostal believers.

The pinnacle for all Pentecostals, though, is not Kansas or Texas, but California. It was in Los Angeles on Azusa Street that a Black man, William J. Seymour, led an integrated group on an historic occasion. At this "American Jerusalem" as Vinson Synan calls it, at a time when prejudicial concepts and segregation still reigned supreme, Blacks and whites experienced speaking in tongues in a way that had been exceeded only by the initial experience.

The 1906 experience is vital in the history of the Pentecostal movement. In the Pentecostal-Apostolic movement, however, a subsequent experience in 1913 holds equal significance. For this experience, which has helped to distinguish the Apostolics from other Pentecostals, led to the belief that correct baptism is in the "Name of the Lord Jesus Christ." This led to rejection of the traditional Trinitarian formula, as well as rejection of the Trinitarian doctrine.

In his book, *The Pentecostals,* Walter J. Hollenweger offers this helpful information:

> John G. Scheppe, a participant in a Pentecostal camp meeting in Arroyo Seco, California, so rejoiced at the name of Jesus, which had worked miracles in that meeting, that he leapt up for joy and cried out to those at the Camp, 'How great a discovery the glory of the name of Jesus had been to him in that night of prayer.' The slogan was adopted by Glenn A. Cook, Frank Ewart (stalwarts of the white United Pentecostal Church (UPC) and others. They sought to find the significance of the name of Jesus in scripture and discovered that in the Acts of the Apostles, baptism was always 'in the name of Jesus.' ... This showed that preachers who baptized with the trinitarian formula had less authority for they were foolish enough to try and give a better interpretation of the formula of baptism than the Apostles themselves... They

taught that Jesus was the name of God the Father, Son and Holy Spirit.[1]

Along with Cook and Ewart, whom Hollenweger mentions, was a notable Black man not mentioned, Garfield Thomas Haywood, who played a very important role in the formative stages of the Oneness or Apostolic churches. This outstanding biblical scholar eventually became the first presiding bishop of the Pentecostal Assemblies of the World. (This body is the oldest predominately Black Apostolic organization in the world. All others can trace their beginnings back to this group.)

From 1914 to the present, the Apostolic organizations have witnessed countless splits and schisms. With these have come an unbelievable proliferation of bishops to oversee various new groups. This is the contemporary situation. There are, however, historical factors that should be considered that hopefully will help us better understand, if not appreciate, the present predicament of the Black Pentecostal Apostolic church.

The Wesleyan Influence

One factor which should be given some consideration is the influence of John Wesley. This influence has come through the Methodist, Holiness and Pentecostal movements to the Apostolic churches today. It seems to be from John Wesley's theology that much of the doctrine and dogma of this church has evolved and developed. Quite appropriately, then, some effort should be given to

---

[1] Walter Hollenweger, *The Pentecostals* (Minneapolis, Minnesota: Augsburg Publishing House, 1972), pp. 31-32.

see what it was about Wesley's theology that has nurtured to fruition in the Apostolic church.

John Wesley was born in the rectory at Epworth, Lincolnshire, England. He was the fifteenth child of the British, Anglican clergyman, Samuel Wesley and his wife Susannah. Obviously, then, young Wesley himself was nurtured and grew in a Christian religious environment. And in addition to having a father who was a minister, two other very important people in his life became preachers. They were his brother Charles who became a noted hymnist as well, and George Whitefield, who later developed very close ties with Calvinism

Given the circumstances of John Wesley's childhood and developmental years, the escaping of a career in some phase of religion or ministry - seemed fairly improbable. It would not be too much of an error to assume that immense encouragement and guidance filtered down from "Daddy" Wesley to have his sons pursue a similar profession. As a matter of fact, John even served as his father's assistant at one time.

Ordained deacon in 1725 and admitted to the priesthood of the Church of England in 1728, John Wesley acted for a time as curate to his father.[2] After a short tenure with his father, John Wesley, along with his brother Charles and good friend George Whitefield, entered Lincoln College at Oxford. The initial year of entrance for John Wesley was 1725. While at Lincoln College, membership in a rather interesting club seemed to have had subsequent historical significance. While there, meaning in attendance at the college, Wesley joined the

---

[2] *Funk and Wagnall's New Encyclopedia,* Vol 25, p. 48.

Holy Club, a group of students that included his brother Charles, and George Whitefield... The club members adhered strictly and methodically to religious precepts and practices, among them visiting prisons and comforting the sick, and were thus derisively called 'methodists' by their schoolmates." [3] The term eventually became the designated name of the denomination that claims Wesley as its founder and father, the Methodist Church.

If one takes the time to scrutinize great or leading figures in history, two points of interest can be noted, among whatever others are there. First, many of life's outstanding personalities had messages that were prophetic and hence led to their rejection. by many of their contemporaries and constituencies. To just name three: Jesus, Mahatma Gandhi, and Martin Luther King, Jr. would appear to me to fit this category. Secondly, many of the outstanding personalities appeared to be in search of something else beyond the normal life pursuits of their times. (One is moved to shake out of the oft-time narrow confinement of the status quo or establishment-oriented traditionalism.) With a fervor and a zeal surpassed by few, Saul of Tarsus seemed to hunger and thirst for a spiritual insight that was uncharacteristic of many Jews at that time. Because of the desire to become fully open to God's use, it happened for him on the way to Damascus. John Wesley, it may be assumed, had a desire to achieve holiness to a degree unknown at that period.

Among some of the books that Wesley read during his formative year-s were those by William Law. The sincere

---

[3] Ibid., pp. 48-49.

young cleric thought highly of *Law's Treaties on Christian Perfection and Serious Call to a Devout and Holy Life.*

Reading Serious Call in 1725, Wesley adopted much of Law's thought as his own. In this book Law called for a holiness of life in the laity which the church for centuries had reserved only for the monastics and clergy. 'For there is no reason,' wrote Law, 'why you should think the highest holiness, the most heavenly tempers, to be the duties and happiness of a bishop, but what is as good a reason why you should think the same tempers to be the duty and happiness of all Christians.'[4]

Vinson Synan contends that the remainder of Wesley's life was spent in the pursuit of the holiness of heart that Law had articulated in his writings.

Many of the Wesley biographers attach significant meaning to Wesley's trip to the colony of Georgia in America. That trip took place in 1735. Coming to a British colonial satellite, this Anglican missionary felt inspired to help save the European immigrants as well as the native Indians. Because his preaching emerged from a belief in strict principles of conduct, little enthusiasm was forthcoming from the American whites. The American Indians likewise lacked the interest in learning which Wesley emphasized. Although there is general consensus among Wesleyan writers that his stay in America was largely unproductive and unsuccessful, there is agreement that the trip itself meant much to John Wesley. For it gave him an opportunity to meet some Moravian Pietists. It

---

[4] Vinson Synan, *The Holiness Pentecostal Movement In The United States* (Grand Rapids, Michigan: William B. Eerdman's Publishing Co., 1971), pp. 14-15.

seems that when the storms on the sea caused many aboard to become fearful, the Pietists maintained a mature calm that was grounded in their religious belief. Their faith in God was enough assurance that the ship would safely and satisfactorily reach the distant shores of the southern colony of Georgia. Having felt some discomfort and apprehension himself, Wesley desired to achieve a similar point of maturity in his own spiritual life. His dissatisfaction with his own level of religious maturity and a largely fruitless missionary journey, proved to be enough to send John Wesley back to England.

How well Wesley must have remembered his first encounter with the Moravians. For upon his return to his native homeland, he sought diligently to locate some of this group for further encounter. This second meeting resulted in the experience for Wesley that many of the Holiness movements called an experience of sanctification. This "new experience" for Wesley took place on Aldersgate Street in London, England. The date was May 24, 1738.

> Mr. Hall, Kinchin, Ingham, Whitefield, Hutchins, and my brother Charles, were present at our love-feast in Fetter-Lane, with about sixty of our brethren. About three in the morning, as we were continuing instant in prayer, the power of God came mightily upon us, inasmuch that many cried out for exceeding joy, and many fell to the ground. As soon as we recovered a little from that awe and amazement at the presence of His Majesty, we broke out with one voice, 'We praise Thee, o God; we acknowledge Thee to be the Lord.'[5]

---

[5] Ibid., p. 17.

In the minds of many, this experience is paramount because it is here that Wesley first began to really understand what it meant to be saved by grace. He could now speak from a personal experience. Further some contend that Wesley's ideas on salvation with a prime emphasis on sanctification began to take shape subsequent to this Aldersgate Street experience.

On the other hand, Harold Lindstrom, a Wesleyan scholar, reports that others among Wesleyan scholars have contended that 1725 is more correctly the year of the initial change in the theological development of John Wesley.

Ought we not perhaps to make 1725 the really important turning point, when at Oxford, under the influence of practical mysticism, Wesley was first inspired by his ideal of sanctification?

If we do this, 1738 becomes only the culmination of a process dating from 1725.[6]

This is the view that is espoused by Leger and Piette. But additionally, Lindstrom presents the argument of Rattenbury. Rattenbury does not minimize the significance of Wesley's conversion, as he described it. "It meant a rediscovery of God and was the foundation-stone of 'the permanent historical values of the Evangelical Revival.'[7] "

---

[6] Harold Lindstrom, *Wesley and Sanctification* (London: The Epworth Press, 1950), p. 8.
[7] Ibid., p. 9.

The list could continue with writers taking opposing views on the significance of the years 1725 and 1738. At the end there would still simply be opposing views. The point here is to arrive at a position of salvation emphasizing sanctification that filtered down through Methodism, the Holiness movement, Pentecostalism, and into the doctrine of the Black Apostolic church.

Synan gives us a good point of departure. He feels that by 1740 Wesley's ideas on theology were fairly well set, in terms of shaping the Methodist movement, "... they involved two separate phases of experience for the believer: the first, conversion or justification, and second, Christian perfection, or sanctification."[8] Some definitions for justification and sanctification may be helpful at this point.

In its general usage, justification is being made righteous; showing or being shown to be in the right, or at least blameless. It also means being put right with God. If; as many teach, people are not by nature righteous, but sinful, then one can only be put right by finding pardon and acceptance with God. Alan Richardson provides more definitive statements:

> In classical protestant theology, man is justified by faith alone, or more precisely by grace through faith in Christ alone. In classical usage, it is more important to realize that the word alone is meant to exclude all thought of sinful man's doing or deserving; all works and merits of his, as in any way motivating his justification.

---

[8] Synan, *op. cit.,* p. 18.

In Protestantism after Luther, justification came to be thought of simply as the forgiveness of non-imputation of sin, while renewal of life through the Holy Spirit (sanctification) was a quite distinct and even separate gift.[9]

Sanctification in its classical definition means making or being made holy. According to Richardson, "Holiness is the peculiar and distinctive characteristic of God and of all that is specially associated with God." Th us ancient Israel and the Christian church as the people of God are a 'holy nation' (Exodus 19:6; I Peter 2:9). And all members arc saints; holy ones. The author continues with the following:

The supreme standard and pattern of holiness is Jesus Christ. God intends his people to be conformed to the image of his Son. Holiness is Christlikeness, which the spirit effects in us from one degree of glory to another (II Corinthians 3:18). [10]

The foregoing are classical definitions of justification and sanctification. On the other hand, Wesley has two definitions that relate to what the writer is addressing himself in this book. Briefly stated, *justification* is what God does for us through His Son. *Sanctification* is what He works in us by His Spirit. So then, with these concepts being emphasized, a new movement was really underway.

It has been stated that a movement is never preconceived. It arises in answer to a real problem and

---

[9] Alan Richardson, ed., *Dictionary of Christian Theology* (Philadelphia: Westminster Press, 1969), pp. 184-185.
[10] Ibid., p. 303.

offers itself as an attempt toward a real solution. From this one can assume that very real circumstances led to the Wesleyan revival in the eighteenth century. A minimal amount of research will reveal that this particular time in history witnessed the growth and development of a rationalistic and deistic philosophy. Perhaps because of the accompanying scientific advancement, deism really had its opportunity. Among the main tenets, deists held that reason itself was capable of demonstrating validity for believing in God. There was no need for divine revelation; for the answer was obtainable through natural science.

This seems to be a position theologically similar to that formerly held by the Nation of Islam when it was headed by Elijah Muhammad, headquartered in Chicago, Illinois. (They are now known as the American Muslim Mission headed by Warith Deen Muhammad.) If one understood their doctrine correctly, they concluded that God was a man whose proper name was Allah. Allah possessed the highest, the supreme intelligence of anyone who had lived on this earth. Further they believed that religion was a science that was as exact as mathematics. There was according to the Black Muslims, no such things as "spooks." This was their word for the Christian usage of the term Holy Spirit. Just as the case was with the deists in the eighteenth century, so with the Nation of Islam there was no room for revelation from the spirit of God. Under Warith Deen Muhammad, however, the doctrinal position espoused by his father the late Elijah Muhammad, has changed.

Since naturalistic philosophy was in vogue about the time that the Wesleyan revival commenced, what was the response of Wesley and his followers to this bold new interpretation in religion? The fact is the Wesleyan movement made no effort to deal with attacks by deism. Wesley felt that he and his followers should merely continue expressing their faith in the Bible as the word of God. Wesley even ignored these opponents in his writings. This was somewhat of a new tactic because others attempted to be Christian apologists. This voice of faith in the midst of those of reason served to revive and rekindle the Christian tradition as many knew it previously.

In addition to deism experiencing its zenith around the commencement of the Wesleyan revival, another factor also came into play. The Wesleyan movement emerged as the moral counterpart to the immoral and corrupt tendencies of the eighteenth century in England.

> The new movement in politics and the novel chances for increasing wealth had gone a long way in producing a general indifference to all questions of religious life. The statesmen and scholars of the time paid little attention to religion; and drunkenness and foul talk were not held to be a discredit... Marriage vows were no longer kept sacred, and (a) Lord Chesterfield instructed his son in the art of seduction as a mark of a gentleman.[11]

The corruption at that time pervaded the political and governmental system, while immorality was tearing families asunder. It did not stop there. The slave trade was encouraged by the leaders of the nation.

---

[11] William R. Cannon, *The Theology of John Wesley* (New York: Abingdon-Cokesbury Press, 1946), p. 23.

...As late as 1775 Lord Dartmouth, the Secretary of State for the colonies and one of the most conspicuous leaders in English, religious life exclaimed in regard to slavery: 'We cannot allow the colonies to check or discourage in any degree a traffic so beneficial to the nation.'[12]

To compound matters, at a time when help should have been forthcoming from the church, according to William Cannon, the church was spiritually impotent for the task. Because many in church positions were simply political appointees, autonomy and spirituality were passé.

These then were the conditions that at least helped to stir and ignite the Wesleyan revivals. The agenda had already been prepared. Wesley set about preaching on the theme of righteousness. Here we have an abbreviated version of how the Wesleyan movement got started in Europe. And it is important to remember that from this theme of righteousness that Wesley preached, there was heavy emphasis on what he called "Scriptural Christianity." This really amounted to the beginning of his doctrine of sanctification. For by scriptural Christians, Wesley meant persons who ascribed to an inward and outward holiness way of life. The important thing was not so much to discuss theology but rather to live wholesome, clean, decent lives; "to become in actuality 'lively portraits' of Him whom ye are appointed to represent among men."[13]

The doctrine of sanctification may be seen as taking shape as the "second blessing" of grace. Conversion, of

---

[12] Ibid., pp. 23-24.
[13] Ibid., p. 25.

course, is the first. There have been lengthy discussions in terms of how Wesley understood exactly when sanctification took place. One may agree with Lindstrom who feels that the most accurate understanding of sanctification must be looked at in light of Wesley's concept of sin and atonement.

In dealing first with the concept of sin, one is on safe grounds to say that Wesley held to the depravity of man. All mankind, according to Wesley, was (is) born in sin. This of course resulted from the fall of Adam.

> Man was created looking directly to God, as his last end; but, falling into sin, he fell off from God, and turned into himself. Now, this infers a total apostasy and universal corruption in man; for where the last end is changed, there can be no real goodness. And this is the case of all men in their natural state: They seek not God, but themselves. Hence though many fair shreds of morality are among them, yet, there is none that doeth good, no, not one.' For though some of them 'run well,' they are still off the way; they never aim at the right mark. Whithersoever they move, they cannot move beyond the circle of self. They seek themselves, they act for themselves; their natural, civil, and religious, from whatever spring they come, do all run into, and meet in this dead sea.[14]

In terms of original sin, Wesley's position is basically similar to Luther's and Calvin's in terms of man's predicament before conversion. But whereas Calvin's, and

---

[14] Colin W. Williams, *John Wesley's Theology Today* (New York: Abingdon Press, 1950), p. 50.

even Wesley's once intimate colleague George Whitefield, brought in the doctrine of predestination and election, Wesley refuted such a doctrine. Whitefield believed it to be most dishonorable to make man's salvation depend on man's *free will,* rather than God's *free, grace.* John Wesley, however, responded to that by using the term *prevenient grace.* It is through and by prevenient grace, Wesley reasoned, that man is able to hear God's word and see himself. But even after having seen and heard, man still has the freedom to accept or reject *redeeming grace,* which ultimately leads one to salvation.

Essentially, Wesley agreed with Luther on the doctrine of original sin. The depravation through Adam had in fact permeated the whole historical man. Consequently, no one born of woman could be without blemish or without sin. This doctrine has withstood the test of time and is a cardinal point in the doctrine of the twentieth century Black Apostolic church.

On the contrary, Wesley's attitude toward predestination was simply that the doctrine was unfounded and unscriptural. Predestination, as Wesley understood It. alleviates man of any responsibility. God had already made up his mind as to who will be saved and who will be lost. There is no need for people to do anything, because God has done it all. Accepting this doctrine would be tantamount to offering moral laxity. And if there were one thing that Wesley did not condone, loose moral character was that one thing. Predestination was simply unworkable and ludicrously absurd in Wesley's theology.

When one considers the concept of atonement, original sin assumes more importance. For the depravation through Adam is similarly countered by restoration through Christ. The fall, according to Wesley, was the specific condition that necessitated the coming of Christ.

In connection with the Incarnation it is maintained that Christ, who was a true God and a true man, truly suffered, was crucified, dead and buried, to reconcile his Father to us, and to be a sacrifice, not only for original guilt, but also for all actual sins of men... The sacrifice of Christ, 'once made, is that perfect redemption, propitiation, and satisfaction, for all the sins of the whole world both original and actual; and there is none other satisfaction for sin, but that alone.[15]

Relating this as such to the idea of justification, Wesley adds:

Thus, justification is bound up with three related factors: from God, His mercy and grace; from Christ, His satisfaction of God's justice by the ransom of His blood and His perfect fulfillment of the law; and from man: a true and living faith in the merits of Christ, a faith which is yet not his own work but God's working in him. Through faith man relies on the promise of God's mercy and the forgiveness of sins. Thus, any idea of man achieving justification due to merits resulting from any action of his own is entirely eliminated. [16]

---

[15] Lindstrom, op. cit., p. 60.
[16] Ibid., pp. 63-64.

This understanding of the atonement seems to fit alongside most traditional views. The task for man within this perspective is to freely respond to redeeming grace. When one chooses to make the response according to Wesley, the person is undergoing the conversion experience. It is not necessarily a calm, peaceful experience, as many of the early American Methodist would verify. It is the recognition of one's conscious sinful state coupled with the intentionality to change. This was considered the first work of grace.

Sanctification is the subsequent transformation of the heart and life of the person, according to Wesley. The essence of this change is love.

If one must use labels, it is difficult to believe that Wesley underwent what would be described as a sanctification experience at Aldersgate. He became aware that holiness and moral discretion could be practiced in this life. Sanctification, although considered to "be attained instantly as a 'second work of grace,' was usually preceded and followed by a gradual 'growth in grace.' [17] Sanctification as the second work of grace was the "new thing" that was peculiar to Methodism when it was brought to the shores of America.

With the Virginia colony as its primary base of operation, the Methodist Church in America began to experience unparalleled growth and success in the new country. Behind the leadership of such personalities as Thomas Webb, Thomas Coke, Richard Wright, and

---

[17] Synan, *op cit.,* p. 19.

Francis Asbury, the new movement forged its way into acceptance in the new world.

The emphasis on a "personal experience kind of religion" that allowed freedom of emotional expression was a marked contrast to the liturgical churches that dotted settlements throughout the colonial communities.

The early Methodists successfully combined revivals and circuit ministry as avenues for reaching hundreds of people in the towns and the rural backwoods. As the Methodist Church began to grow, rather than providing In alternative to churches that it had first criticized, a similarity began to develop. The warm, free spirited, and joyful Methodists were also becoming staid and institutionalized.

Many of the old Methodist preachers were shocked by the "new breed" minister. Many of this new breed had been trained in Germany. Therefore, many had been opposed to higher criticism of biblical scripture. This resulted in questions as to the validity of literal interpretation of the Bible. This bold, audacious attitude naturally sent shock waves through the minds of many Wesleyan Methodists. The resulting backlash eventually led to new church denominations.

The Holiness Movement Is Born

Because of dissatisfaction with the new breed of ministers, a number of Methodists played a dominant role in the Holiness movement. But according to two Pentecostal authors, social conditions also served to spur growth of the new movement. Morris E. Golder, historian for the Pentecostal Assemblies of the World, states:

> There were those who felt that the major churches were slipping, slowly but surely, into the realm of modernism; abandoning the true faith for concepts of rationalism and materialism... The Holiness movement was central in this massive move.
>
> The social conditions of America which were deplorable after the Civil War, corruption in politics, and the rise in individual vice, ... were vigorously opposed by the Holiness movement.[18]

Vinson Synan seems to concur with Golder's observation with supportive statements of his own:

> The fact that the Holiness and Pentecostal movements arose during the same period that such intellectual currents as Darwinism, higher criticism, the social gospel, and the ecumenism of the Federal Council of Churches were gaining ascendancy in much of Protestantism, demands an analysis of relationships... In leaving the older churches, the holiness people were protesting against these modernistic developments and were attempting to keep alive the 'old time religion.'[19]

Synan continues by showing that the would-be benefactors of the social gospel rejected this offer of help:

---

[18] Morris E. Golder, *History of the Pentecostal Assemblies of the World* Indianapolis, Indiana, 1973), pp. 6-7.

[19] Synan, *op cit.,* p. 57.

Interestingly enough, he says, the very groups that the social gospel wished to help, the poor, the destitute, and the underprivileged, were the very ones who ... most bitterly denounced the Gladdens and the Rauschenbusch leaders of the social gospel movement.[20]

Synan suggests that dancing, cigarettes, and liquor were considered by those in the Holiness movement to be far greater sins than poverty or inequality.

The Holiness movement in its genesis was inter-denominational in character. As such there were no plans at the outset to start a whole new denomination. One of the major tenets was to give heightened emphasis to Wesley's concept of sanctification. Somewhere along the line, the Holiness groups felt that the institutionalized church had forgotten about this important aspect of spiritual living.

There were numerous groups that eventually aligned themselves with the Holiness movement. But according to one source the actual beginning took place at a camp meeting in 1867.

> The real fact is that the call for this vineland, camp meeting was called by thirteen Methodist ministers of New York. The meeting was to be July 17-26, 1867. The group named themselves, 'The National Camp Meeting Association for the Promotion of Christian Holiness.' The camp meeting was-held for the promotion of the work of entire sanctification. Believing in the' literal

---

[20]Ibid., p. 60.

interpretation of the Bible, the group strove for the moral perfection of believers; it also believed in the three works of grace.[21]

This last part of the preceding quotation is vitally important because for the first time there is mention of a third work of grace. Heretofore, two experiences: conversion and sanctification had been marked out.

This Vineland. New Jersey camp meeting was directed by W, Osborn, A. Cockman and J. Inskip, according to Prudcncio Damboriena. The camp meeting later shortened its name to National Holiness Association. The following passage sharpens the issue:

> The machinery ... was already in operation and could have easily been transformed into a particular denomination of more than one million members. The delegates ... asked for such a step, but leaders steadfastly counseled against "come-outism" and directed the delegates to remain loyal to their denominations. However, this insistence on loyalty caused the movement to fragment, as groups in different annual conferences left the churches piecemeal in disputes over local conditions.[22]

In addition to Methodists, persons from the Baptist and Presbyterian churches also ascribed to the doctrines of sanctification and joined the Holiness movement. It is maintained, however, that with heavy emphasis on the Wesleyan sanctification concept, the movement probably

---

[21] Golder, op. cit., p. 9.
[22] Prudencio Damboriena, *Tongues As of Fire* (Washington, D.C.: Corpus Books, 1969), pp. 22-23.

had its greatest appeal among Methodists. After all, such terminology was not foreign to them. It gave them a sense of returning to their primary faith and conviction.

As the Holiness movement continued to grow, primarily in the rural South and mid-West, its unofficial leaders periodically met with the leadership of the Methodist church to discuss their differences. Methodists felt that if the holiness people were pursuing the same objectives, then there was no need for a separate organization. The feeling was summed up in these statements:

> We do not question the sincerity and zeal of these brethren. We desire the church to profit by their earnest preaching and godly example. But we deplore their teaching and method in so far as they claim a monopoly of the experience, practice and advocacy of holiness, and the fact that they separate themselves from the body of our ministers and discipline.[23]

Rather than healing the rift, these words served to escalate the points of difference. Holiness people began to feel that they had been read out of the Methodist Church.

Subsequently what had been a movement entered the rapidly growing phase of a new denomination. One of the first church bodies to come into existence under the holiness heading was the Fire-Baptized Holiness Church. The founder was Benjamin Hardin Irwin of Lincoln, Nebraska. One of the major beliefs of this body was the experience of sanctification. But Irwin went a step further. "Having already been sanctified, Irwin began to seek the

---

[23] Ibid., p. 25.

'baptism of fire' for himself. Eventually he received such an experience which came to him with great ecstasy and demonstrations of joy.[24]" It was immediately after this experience that Irwin began to preach the third experience, the baptism of the spirit.

All of the holiness churches did not accept Irwin's "new theory." Others still maintained that the second blessing, sanctification, was also the baptism with the Holy Spirit. This group held that no third blessing was needed or necessary; sanctification was the ultimate experience.

Irwin's third step eventually led to yet another movement beyond Holiness:

The Fire-Baptized Holiness Church played an important role in helping to lay the foundation for the modern Pentecostal Movement. It taught and emphasized that the baptism of the Holy Ghost was a separate experience subsequent to sanctification, thus laying the basic doctrinal base for the coming Pentecostal movement... In the social, doctrinal, and intellectual sense, the Fire-Baptized Holiness Church was a direct precursor of the modern Pentecostal movement. [25]

In terms of historical development, that part of the church movement that held sanctification to be a real personal experience. has steadily evolved. From the Anglican Church of England, Wesley and followers

---

[24] Synan, *op. cit.,* p. 13.
[25] Golder, *op. cit.,* p. 13.

spearheaded the Wesleyan revivals. Taking on the name Methodist the group continued to grow after being transplanted to the United States. A deemphasis on sanctification by the then affluent Methodist church resulted in the development of the Holiness movement; later the Holiness denominations.

The religious climate, as the nineteenth century drew to a close, was one of spiritual expectation and anticipation. People had demonstrated, time and again, that they wanted more of God's grace. They only wanted to know how could the same be obtained? This was one of the reasons why the different movements kept getting responses to their distinctive and peculiar messages. People were anxious and hopeful of receiving even more from God.

Pentecost: "The Modern Genesis"

Most Pentecostal writers agree that the contemporary movement really started with Charles Fox Parham in Topeka, Kansas in 1901. Starting with Parham does not at all eliminate or refute the fact that groups prior to him had the Pentecostal experience. For it is noted that:

Before the Pentecostal movement sprang into being there existed in the United States scattered instances of individuals and small groups who had experienced an ecstatic spirit baptism manifested by speaking with tongues... But only from the beginning of 1901 can we speak of a real Pentecostal Movement, and even this movement was rather unassuming and localized until April 1906. [26]

---

[26] Nils Block-Hoell, *The Pentecostal Movement* (Oslo:

Charles Parham, originally with the Congregational Church, became a Methodist. He later developed close ties with branches of the Holiness movement. His experiences with these people, along with the Methodist teaching of sanctification, aroused his concern and interest in glossolalia. At a later stage, Parham (as a result of his belief) began to teach that speaking in tongues should be a normative Christian experience. Obviously, this was not the prevailing opinion toward glossolalia at that time. Some looked on speaking in tongues as a strange, meaningless incident that happened long ago. For many, the experience had no contemporary significance.

In an effort to deal more in depth with his new teaching, Parham opened a school in October, 1900, in Topeka, Kansas. Starting with thirty to forty students, it was called Bethel Bible College. Because of the heavy emphasis on literal interpretation of scripture, "the Bible was considered the only textbook necessary and thus, the only one used."[27]

A few days prior to the Christmas holidays in 1900, Parham prepared to leave so that he could be involved in religious services in other sections of Kansas. He gave his students an assignment to work on during his absence. Believing that there was another work of grace subsequent to sanctification, Parham assigned the students the "Baptism of the Holy Ghost" as a subject. The object was to see if there were any biblical evidence given for a doctrine of the Holy Ghost.

Universitets Forlaget, 1964)
[27] Golder, *op. cit.,* p. 17.

Using the book of Acts as their source of study, the students surprised Parham by their conclusions. All of the students agreed that speaking in tongues was the one sign that accompanied each occasion of this charismatic experience. This opinion was later adopted by Pentecostals as a biblical fact of monumental importance. According to Morris Golder, the remarkable conclusion reached by Parham and his students was the first time that speaking in tongues had ever been considered 'as the initial physical evidence of a person's having received the baptism of the Holy Ghost.

After embarking on a rather extensive revival crusade, that was carried on periodically for over four years, Parham and some of his followers headed for the Lone Star state. On July 10, 1905, the group of Pentecostal seekers arrived in Houston, Texas. Because many of the "curious and the serious" were being attracted to this new message, Parham decided to open another school in Houston. Known as "The Bible. Training School," it operated tuition free.

It was at this school in Houston that the first notable Black personalities were involved in this new movement.

. William J. Seymour, a Black preacher who was blind in one eye, had moved to Texas. A native of Louisiana, the Baptist minister had developed strong holiness leanings. fie was also a man with a progressive mind, because after hearing of Parham's school, he sought to enroll to improve his religious training. Here it is noted that:

The racial mores of the South dictated that Seymour, a Negro could not attend Parham's school. However, his great desire to attend classes and his apparent thirst for

WITH WATER AND SPIRIT

knowledge led Parham to allow him to attend the Bible classes during the day... He was taught that the holiness movement had been wrong in asserting that sanctification was also the baptism with the Holy Spirit. It was rather a 'third experience' separate in time and nature from the 'second blessing.' Sanctification cleansed and purified the believer, while the baptism with the Holy Spirit brought great power for service.[28]

The school continued to attract many visitors. Houston residents even carried their out-of-town guests to the Bible Training School. One such guest helped to further spread this Pentecostal message. Sister Neely Terry went to the school while visiting friends in Houston. While there she began to speak in tongues and rejoice. Soon after, Sister Terry returned to Los Angeles, her home. There she enthusiastically related the details of this new Pentecostal experience. This resulted in a group of people inviting William J. Seymour to come West with the "new word."

Brother Seymour arrived' in Los Angeles in April, 1906. Here he preached his first sermon from Acts 2:4:

Here begins the modern genesis of the movement. When he (Seymour) arrived in Los Angeles, Seymour gathered a body of Negro saints into homes and later into the refurbished lumber store that became the Azusa Mission to pray for a recurrence of Apostolic signs and miracles. 'Then it happened: multitudinous gifts, signs and manifestations-including tongue-speaking, heralded the advent of the Spirit. For days, these black saints shouted and spoke in tongues while others were

---

[28] Vinson Synan, *op. cit.,* pp. 103-104.

converted or healed... Soon in a kind of reverse desegregation, white people began attending and receiving the same experiences through the ministry of the blacks who led the meetings. [29]

It is interesting to note that in the early twentieth century, when prejudicial ideas and segregation still reigned supreme, both sexes and both races shared this glorious, historical experience and spoke in tongues.

As word of this spiritual "happening" in California spread, more people from other sections of the country began to go westward. Charles H. Mason, a small Black preacher, who had been active in the Holiness movement, heard "bout the Azusa Mission and went to California. (Mason founded and served as the first Presiding Bishop of the Church of God in Christ.) After experiencing speaking in tongues, Mason returned to his Memphis, Tennessee headquarters, jubilantly telling the good news. The church body, after some disagreement, and a small split, agreed to reorganize as a Pentecostal denomination. The Mason-led Church of God in Christ became the first Pentecostal church headquartered in the South to receive official government recognition. Seeing the advantage of this, many white ministers came to Mason to get credentials and ordination. They refused, however, to align themselves officially with Mason's church, which began to grow at an astronomical rate. Today, the Church of God in Christ has over 400,000 members. It is widely considered to be the largest Black Pentecostal church headquartered in the United States.

---

[29] James S. Tinney, "Black Origins of the Pentecostal Movement," *Christianity Today* (October 8, 1971).

Yet Another Development

Thus far, it has been the writer's desire to show how Methodism emerged from the Anglican Church and John Wesley. As a result of dissatisfaction with a de-emphasis on sanctification, the Holiness movement then got started. From that evolved the "third work of grace" people who eventually brought forth the contemporary Pentecostal church. But there is yet another movement that has developed. Essentially this is an extension of the Pentecostal church. This group has become known by its members as the Apostolic church. Others refer to it as Oneness Pentecostals or "Jesus *Only*" churches.

According to Morris *Golder,* the Apostolic church had its beginning at a camp meeting in California:

A Worldwide Pentecostal Camp Meeting with Mary Woodworth Etter as the main speaker, was in progress in Arroyo Seco, California. Many miracles were wrought through the wonderful name of Jesus. One man, John G. Scheppe, was so inspired that he spent the night in prayer. *Along* toward morning he was given a glimpse of the power of that *blessed* name. Leaping to his feet he ran through the camp, shouting to all the early risers what the Lord had shown him. The 'revelation' made a profound impression upon the campers, and all rejoiced with Scheppe, and began to search the Scriptures concerning the name of Jesus. [30]

This experience *resulted* in the belief that water baptism *could only* be administered "in the name of the Lord Jesus Christ." The trinitarian formula was thought to be in error. Eventually the doctrine of the trinity was

[30] Golder, *op. cit.,* pp. 40-41.

refuted as being unbiblical. Apostolics further contended that for the dispensation of grace, Jesus is God. This group saw Jehovah of the *Old* Testament as being Jesus of the New Testament.

Just as the Pentecostal movement started as an integrated group, so too did the Apostolic movement. *Glenn* A. Cook, Frank Ewart (two whites) and Garfield Thomas Haywood, a *Black* minister, emerged as three of the leading personalities in the infant stage of the new Apostolic movement.

It was *only* fitting that the first church organization under the "Jesus Only" banner, was integrated. This group was the Pentecostal Assemblies of the World (PAW). When the first seven bishops were *elected* to oversee this church, four were *Black* and three were white. Bishop G. T. Haywood of Indianapolis, Indiana, became the first presiding bishop.

Because of the feeling that they could better evangelize the world as a separate group, the majority of whites split from PAW in 1924 to form their own Apostolic church. In addition to the racial split, there have been many splits among Blacks. These splits resulted because of doctrinal differences, administrative differences, and what appears to be impatient, ambitious leaders. The late Bishop Robert C. Lawson, founder of the Church of Our Lord Jesus Christ of the Apostolic Faith, was the first person to split from PAW on a doctrinal difference. The following is suggestive of tensions:

In 1919 the great question of marriage and divorce had caused no small stir... and one of the outstanding men,

Elder Robert C. Lawson left the organization. Along with his disagreement with the PAW's stand on the marriage and divorce issue was also Elder Lawson's disagreement with the organization's stand on the freedom of women in the ministry.[31]

The proliferation of splits and new organizations has produced a countless number of bishops to head the various church groups. Although each new group might have a new interpretation on some particular point, there is a strand of commonality. In the midst of all this diversity, all agree that:

1.All believers must be baptized in water in the name of the Lord Jesus Christ, and,

2.All believers must receive the Holy Ghost, with speaking in tongues as the accompanying initial evidence.

---

[31] *Ibid.,* pp. 93-94.

CHAPTER II
WE MULTIPLY BY DIVIDING

Many people have said that American Blacks are too splintered. They have generally referred to the failure of Blacks to get involved in the mainstream of American life. It has been generally believed that too much sectionalism, focus on personalities, and inability to reach consensus on diverse ideologies have been some of the significant reasons for minimal progress. It must be added, however, that these faults of Blacks themselves have not by any means been the only reasons group potential has not been more fully realized. Certainly, the manifestations of white racism have conspicuously presented many deterrents to progress.

There are, nonetheless, some areas of Black life where the blame for retrogression cannot easily be laid on racism. One of those areas is Black religion. Under this heading one can note the Black Apostolic Church. If beliefs of this church in water baptism in Jesus' name, and receiving the Holy Ghost with speaking in tongues have been points of agreement, then splits and schisms hove revealed other characteristics of disunity. Since that day in 1919, when Robert C. Lawson expressed a doctrinal difference with the church hierarchy of the Pentecostal Assemblies of the World and left that fellowship, the trend has continued unabated. Lawson's departure from

PAW resulted in his founding the Church of Our Lord Jesus Christ of the Apostolic Faith (COOLJC). From that day to the present, Black Apostolics have been multiplying by dividing. And unless some revolutionary changes take place in the mentality and attitudes of many church leaders, more divisions will continue.

This then is the problem. To leave it there would be truly unfair when one thinks of trying to offer possible solutions. In the interest of solutions, it might be helpful o mark out the extent of the problem. This will be done by listing the births of some Black Apostolic organizations Only about 21 will be listed, for two reasons. First, the writer's knowledge of all the organizations is incomplete. He learns of other groups nearly every year. For there are new groups formed almost every year. Secondly, the time that would be needed for travel and research to discover all of the Black Apostolic organizations is not available. It is believed, however, that the organizations that will be mentioned, because of their size and geographical boundaries, will certainly be more than an adequate sampling. In addition to the organizations that will be mentioned (representing approximately 2,70S congregations and 1.4 million members in America and abroad.) Other Black Apostolic organizations include:

The Glorious Church of God in Christ Apostolic
Bishop Perry Lindsey, Presiding Bishop
Headquarters: Roanoke, Virginia

Powerhouse of Deliverance Church
Bishop J. H. Covington, Presiding Bishop
Headquarters: Greensboro, North Carolina

Greater Emmanuel Apostolic Church, Inc.
Bishop Quander Wilson, Presiding Bishop
Headquarters: Portsmouth, Ohio

Emmanuel Tabernacle Baptist Church (Apostolic)
Bishop Gentry, Presiding Bishop
Headquarters: Columbus, Ohio

Faith Tabernacle Corporation of Churches
Bishop L. W. Osborne, Sr., Presiding Bishop
Headquarters: Portland, Oregon

Holy Temple Church of Christ, Inc.
Bishop Joseph Weathers, Presiding Bishop
Headquarters: Washington, DC.

Free Gospel Church of Christ, Inc.
Bishop Ralph Green, Presiding Bishop
Headquarters: Coral Hills, Maryland

Victory Pentecostal Apostolic Church, Inc.
Bishop R. H. Prince, Presiding Bishop
Headquarters: Landover, Maryland

Macedonia Churches of Virginia
Bishop Tilman Carmichael, Sr., Presiding Bishop
Headquarters: Gloucester, Virginia

New Apostolic Association of Baltimore, Maryland
Bishop Morris R. Lane, President
Headquarters: Baltimore, Maryland

Living Witness of Apostolic Faith, Inc.
Bishop Charles E. Poole, Presiding Bishop
Headquarters: Chicago, Illinois

As one reads this section, it should be remembered that many of the traditional denominations are uniting or moving toward merger. Will Apostolic organizations ever change the trend of divisions and begin to unite? This writer hopes that Apostolic churches will come to realize the strength of a united ministry.

The organizations listed below are arranged in chronological order, in so far as possible. Where groups were formerly known by a different name, the date of the originally-named organization will be used. Where founders previously were members of a preceding group, but left to begin their own organization, the date of the latter organization will be used.

The Church of God (Apostolic)
1897

The Church of God (Apostolic) was organized at Danville, Kentucky in the year 1897, by Elder Thomas J. Cox. "At that time, it was called the Christian Faith Band; under which name it was later incorporated (in 1901) at the General Assembly, held at Freeman, West Virginia," says its *Discipline.*[1]

The early history of the Church of God (Apostolic) predated the American contemporary Apostolic movement. Before Cox became Apostolic, he met and worked with R. C. Lawson. During this period Elder Cox was baptized in the name of the Lord Jesus Christ, and also received the Holy Ghost.

---

[1] Eli Neal, *Discipline of the Church of God (Apostolic). s.l.: s.n., s.d.,* p. 3.

After several years of using the church name Christian Faith Band, some questions arose about the possibility of" a church name that had a biblical connection. The church Discipline notes that on "August 15, 1915, the General Overseer held a council with the Board of Elders, concerning the name of the church. The desire was expressed for a more scriptural name. The council recommending that the name of the church be changed to the Church of God (Apostolic) was adopted by more than a two-thirds vote of the assembly. The latter, however, seeing that a number desired to hold the old name, did not press the matter, and the church was not incorporated under the new name until 1919 at Paris, Kentucky.[2]

Bishop Thomas J. Cox was obviously a man of considerable fortitude, for this venerable gentleman held the chief position in the Church of God (Apostolic) over four decades. From 1897 to 1943 Cox was presiding bishop. At Bishop Cox's death two men became co-presiding bishops. They were Bishop M. Gravely and Bishop E. N. Neal, who were made co-presiding bishops because neither man wanted to serve under the other.

This joint arrangement only lasted for two years. Then Bishop Gravely left his wife and remarried. Feeling that Gravely had no legitimate grounds for leaving, the first Mrs. Gravely went to the Annual Assembly to contest the separation. There she received considerable support. Gravely's area, Beckley, West Virginia, sided with Sister Gravely.

---

[2] Ibid., p. 3.

In a move toward compromise, the general church agreed to let Gravely continue serving as pastor, but demoted him from bishop to elder. Gravely refused the proposition and was disfellowshipped from the Church of God (Apostolic). A fairly lengthy litigation followed, but Gravely also lost that as well as the pastorate of Saint Luke Church in Beckley, West Virginia. According to reports, he never had any success trying to start another independent congregation. He died in the early 1970s.

By 1945 Bishop Eli Neal had solidly entrenched himself as the presiding bishop of the now-growing Church of God (Apostolic). There he remained for 19 years until 1964.

In an effort to find out what outstanding accomplishments took place under the Neal administration, Dr. R. K. Hash, the current General Overseer, was interviewed. Hash talked about the great teaching reputation of Bishop Neal. "He (Neal) instilled the Apostolic doctrine in all of us." Additionally, Bishop Neal was known as a great preacher and pastor. For many years Saint Peter's Church in Winston-Salem, North Carolina, under Neal's pastorate was one of the leading congregations in the southeast. The congregation never managed to build a new edifice despite the fact that one was sorely needed.

There was yet another blessing that God placed on the ministry of the late Bishop Eli Neal. Many persons who served under this pastorate were inspired to enter the gospel ministry. These included many women, years before the trends introduced by the Women's Liberation Movement.

After the death of Bishop Neal, Bishop Love Odom from Tipton, Georgia, assumed the presiding bishopric. According to R. K. Hash, Odom's singular and most important accomplishment was the creation of a national treasury. This allowed the general church to have considerable financial "working capital" to provide assistance for affiliated churches.

Bishop Odom only served two years (1964-1966) before he died. The year 1966 marked the rise to the top of Bishop David E. Smith. This bishop's tenure with the organization went back many years. In fact, Smith had served as general secretary for the national church during the Neal administration. Smith distinguished himself as a leading preacher and teacher in the Church of God (Apostolic). He also served as pastor of St. Luke Church in Beckley, West Virginia, and Holy Tabernacle in Beco, West Virginia.

One of the most significant accomplishments under Smith's administration was the creation of a sinking fund for the Church of God (Apostolic). The 1973 *Minute Book of the Sixty-Ninth Annual Assembly* says, the "purpose of the sinking fund is to create a source of revenue within the church body in order that the National office might become self-sustaining."

In terms of how the funds were to be raised, the 1973 Minute Book informs us:

"Each member of the Church of God Apostolic ...will pay into an escrow fund (the amount of) $10.00 per month for a period of 36 months.

> 1,000 - Membership
> x $10 - Monthly by each member
> $10,000'

x 36-' Per month
$360,000 - Gross income for (the) fund at the end of 36 months."[3]

Concerning this innovative idea for an apostolic church, we are told, "During the first 36 months no money is to be drawn against the fund for any purpose. The reason is to get the full advantage of ... the amount available."[4]

While Bishop Hash would not be specific about the amount presently in the sinking fund, he did say, "We are well on the way toward our goal ($360,000)." Without a doubt, more projects of this kind could be developed were it not for the ever-present, and constant splitting of organizations and churches among Apostolics. Much of the needless duplication of efforts and many years of fruitful productivity gone-for-nothing could be turned around if Apostolics would work together.

In December 1974, Bishop David E. Smith, the fifth presiding bishop and general overseer of the Church of God (Apostolic) died.

Having served as assistant general overseer during the Smith years, Dr. Reuben K. Hash acted as presider until the 1975 General Assembly. At that time, he was officially installed as the sixth general overseer of the Church of God (Apostolic).

---

[3] George M. Hash, ed., *1973 Minute Book of the Church of God Apostolic*, s.l.: Church of God Apostolic. 173, p. 13.
[4] Ibid., pp. 13-14.

As for accomplishments during his administration, Hash said, "I would like to be remembered for my efforts, to evangelize and (help) fill up the empty pews. Building up the size of the' congregations (of the affiliated churches) is the thing that I am trying to do'." Hash still sees, a tremendous need to engage in missionary efforts.

The general church started with headquarters in Danville, Kentucky at the Zion Hill Church of God. In the 1940s the headquarters was moved to, Saint Luke Church, Beckley, West Virginia. Some years later the headquarters were moved to Saint Peter's Church in Winston-Salem, N.C., the current location.

The Church of God (Apostolic) has more than seventy-five elders, ministers, and evangelists; '43 churches in 12 states and approximately 15,000 members. On the board of bishops are Floyd Crawford, W; R. Pannell, George Hash, J. G. King, S. S. Magee, W: J. Fitzgerald, and Robert 1. Wise.

The Pentecostal Assemblies of the World
1906

There have been disagreements among Pentecostal writers relative to the beginning of PAW. Some of the white writers date its beginning subsequent to that of the Assemblies of God, the large white Pentecostal body, in 1914. But answering charges that he left the Assemblies of God to join the Pentecostal Assemblies of the World, Bishop Garfield Thomas Haywood contended that PAW preceded the white group by several years. He stated that PAW was organized in 1906:

The writer (G. T. Haywood) has never been connected with the Assemblies of God as a movement since its organization at Hot Springs, Arkansas, in 1914, but has carried P.A. of W. credentials since 1911. It would be impossible to 'go back' to a place you have never been. The P.A. of W. is older than the Assemblies of God, as a body, by eight (8) years.[5]

Probably where the bone of contention arises is the fact that PAW was reorganized and enlarged as a Oneness or Apostolic body. This, of course, happened after the "John Scheppe experience" in 1913.

According to the writings of Morris Golder, (PAW historian), H. A. Goss, G. T. Haywood, F. J. Ewart, and J. J. Frazee were extremely instrumental in getting PAW started as THE Oneness Church. Of these four men, only Haywood was black. With J. J. Frazee, serving as the first general superintendent, the Pentecostal Assemblies of the World started developing as an Apostolic church."

First, the new church disagreed with historical Christendom and said that speaking in tongues was a normative experience. Secondly, P A W went a step beyond other Pentecostals and repudiated 'the doctrine of the Trinity. R. C. Lawson articulate spokesmen of this Apostolic belief. Thirdly, the church had very early been an integrated group. This was done at a time when the idea of integration was far from popular. Fourthly, the church accepted the ordination of women, as well as women serving as pastors.

---

[5] Morris Golder, *op. cit.*, p. 36

As one reads Golder one fact begins to emerge. As more Blacks began to affiliate with the new church, whites began to drop away. Some of the early Blacks listed who developed into stalwarts in their own right were R. C. Lawson, Joseph M. Turpin, P. J. F. Bridges and F. I. Douglas.

Lawson, who was one of the early field superintendents from Columbus, Ohio, was the first notable Black to leave the Pentecostal Assemblies of the World. It seems that PAW was too much of a trailblazer for R. C. Lawson, however. He could not accept women clergy nor the PAW stand on divorce and remarriage. So, he left PAW in 1919. As far as it can be determined, Lawson did not influence any of the ministers to leave with him.

After a merger with the General Association of Apostolic Assemblies, and the transferal of the headquarters from Portland, Oregon to Indianapolis, Indiana, PAW was incorporated in the state of Indiana. This step was taken January 25, 1919 and served to give PAW credibility with the government. Further, it served to put the opposition to the new movement on notice that PA W planned to be around for a while.

No doubt this move helped strengthen the influential; position of G. T. Haywood. Not only did he pastor in Indianapolis, he also had one of the largest congregations associated with the new organization (If today's attitudes in the Black Apostolic church are any indication, then as now, the ministers with the largest churches tend to have the most influence in the various organizations.)

The next five years, 1919-1924, were somewhat ambiguous for PAW. While there was growth in terms of the addition of more ministers and new congregations, the race question began to develop into a major problem. The race problem did not just happen. On the contrary, there were early signs pointing toward confrontation. The cognizant individual certainly could detect some of them. Obviously, when it became important for two white presbyters to sign the credentials for the white brethren in the Southland,[6] something was wrong. Even in 1921 it was extremely difficult for a white person to look at. the writings on a white minister's credentials and determine that a Black was the overseer.

The novelty of the initial experiences from 1906 to 1913 were beginning to wear off. The whites were coming to realize that the impending "end" was not going to.be soon. Consequently, the traditional mores of America (including racial segregation) began to become more significant in the minds of the whites. Speaking in tongues, with all the power pertaining thereto, had not been able to subdue the fact that Black was still Black and white was still white, and the two just were not supposed to interact.

The ninth annual convention of the Pentecostal Assemblies of the World met in Chicago, Illinois. The year was 1924. This has since come to be known as the year of the "great split." The whites chose not to be led by the spirit of God that they claimed caused their initial efforts to take place. Instead they gave in to the spirit of tradition, segregation:

---

[6] Ibid., p. 79.

It was at this Convention that all that had been smoldering, broke into open 'fire' dividing-the Pentecostal Assemblies of the World. The Thursday session, October 15, 1924, will always go down in P.A. of W. history as 'infamous as. well as momentous. THE DIVISION HAD COME!!... Elder Haywood was chosen to act as Chairman of this Convention.

... The minutes of the next day carry the account of a 'broken agreement.... The fact that the brethren had separated from us, they had broken their agreement, this body goes on record as not considering them as part of this organization.'

It would be only fair to add that while most of the whites left PAW to form what eventually became the United Pentecostal Church, a minority of whites did remain with PAW.

In the year, 1925, the Pentecostal Assemblies of the World abolished the Board of Presbyters as the governing body. This was replaced by a presiding bishop and a Board of Bishops. In keeping with its efforts to remain as integrated as possible, PA W selected an original board of three whites and four Blacks. They were: G. T. Haywood, first presiding bishop; bishops S. N. Hancock, F. I. Douglas, J. M. Turpin, who were Blacks; and G. B. Rowe, A. William Lewis, and R. G. Pettis, whites. Bishop Haywood remained the head bishop until his death in 1931. Bishop Haywood served this new church as the official head for six years.

Shortly after the death of Bishop Haywood there was an effort led by former white members of PAW, to initiate a merger of the new predominantly white group with PA W. It was felt by some, however, that something less than honesty was a part of the effort. So, it is noted that:

> Most of the brethren of the PAW felt that this was a 'move of God' and were elated, feeling that God again was looking favorably upon the organization. But what seemed at the first to be a blessing really was the trick of Satan.

> In September, 1931, a special call meeting was held in the city of St. Louis, Missouri, for the purpose of attempting a merger of the Pentecostal Assemblies of the World and the Apostolic Churches of Jesus Christ. This meeting was so hastily planned that many of the brethren were not notified of it.[7]

The proposal by the whites was felt to be unfair, in light of the fact that they were the ones who left. After the merger was not effected, the hidden agenda finally came to light:

> Shortly after this attempt at merger, it was found that honesty and sincerity were not the motives behind this attempt. The P.A. of W. Charter was stolen and hidden away; and found in the home of one who did not really know its worth or value. Through the efforts of Bishop A. William Lewis, it was recovered and brought back to its rightful owners.[8]

---

[7] Ibid., p. 6.
[8] Ibid., p. 8.

Although the merger did not work out, the Apostolic Churches of Jesus Christ had some success in wooing several of the Black bishops and elders.

Its ranks somewhat depleted, PA W nevertheless elected a new presiding bishop. This person was entrusted with the task of once again giving leadership and direction to PAW. The man selected for the job came with at least one notable distinction. He was one of the first Black Apostolic missionaries to a foreign land. He had been a missionary in Liberia, West Africa and his name was Samuel Grimes. This great man became one of the outstanding ministers of the Apostolic church. Bishop Grimes held the reigns of leadership from 1932 until his death in 1967, making his tenure a phenomenal thirty-four' years. Because of his very scholarly and knowledgeable approach to scripture, Bishop Grimes helped the Apostolic church gain interdenominational respectability. Many who had considered the group to be a bunch of fanatical "holy rollers," who used religion for some kind of sexual fulfillment, did an about-face after hearing Bishop Grimes. The impression generally given after hearing this physically small-but spiritual giant was "if he were a part of this group, then there must be something that we have overlooked."

The writer remembers quite vividly how one of his undergraduate professors who talked of Bishop Grimes. He conceded that the man had so impressed him in a conversation that if he ever left his church, he would seek to align himself with Bishop Grimes. Such comments were not uncommon with regards to the second presiding bishop of PAW.

WITH WATER AND SPIRIT

But no matter who leads, it is seldom that all those who follow will be satisfied. This seemed to have been the case with Bishop S. N. Hancock of Detroit, Michigan. Although Bishop Hancock had been one of the original seven bishops of PAW, he left in 1957 to form the Pentecostal Churches of the Apostolic Faith Association. Thus, one reads:

> The year 1957 saw another schism in the Pentecostal Assemblies of the World. This schism was not racial in its reason but the result of a power struggle that had existed and smoldered since the death of the late Bishop G. T. Haywood. The late Bishop S. N. Hancock had expressed his feelings after the passing of Bishop Haywood that he should automatically become the presiding bishop.
>
> The struggle came to a head at the General Assembly convening in Baltimore, Maryland, in 1952, when after a heated executive session, there was a run-off vote between Bishop Samuel Grimes and Bishop Samuel Hancock-with Bishop Grimes defeating Bishop Hancock. While Bishop Hancock remained with the PAW until 1957, there was the discontent and disenchantment prevalent.[9]

The church group headed by Hancock thus became the third such group to grow out of the Pentecostal Assemblies of the World. The other two were the Church of the Lord Jesus Christ headed by Bishop Lawson; and the Pentecostal Church, Inc., later becoming the United Pentecostal Church. (This latter one is the white group.)

---

[9] Ibid., p. 141.

Keeping in step with the "multiply by dividing" trend, "the Pentecostal Church of the Apostolic Faith has had at least three schisms since the death of its founder and first presiding Bishop, S. N. Hancock."

The Pentecostal Assemblies of the World continued to move forward. Again, in support of its efforts to remain an integrated group, a white bishop was elected as the assistant presiding bishop. to Bishop Grimes. He was Bishop Ross P. Paddock of Kalamazoo, Michigan. Bishop Paddock assumed the head position at the death of Bishop Grimes. Bishop Frank Bowdan, the Black bishop. of Los Angeles, was subsequently elected the assistant presiding bishop to Bishop Paddock.

As of now, this predominantly Black Apostolic organization has continued to function as an integrated body. Since 1967 it has in fact, been headed by a team of interracial bishops. This is the case in spite of the fact that whites comprise a very small percentage of the entire church.

To get some idea about the contributions of each presiding bishop of PAW, this writer talked with Bishop Morris E. Golder from Indianapolis, Indiana. Golder accepted Christ under the pastorate of Bishop Garfield T. Haywood in 1930. As historian of PAW, Bishop Golder made comments about each of the four presiders.

Starting with the illustrious and revered G. T. Haywood, Golder made these statements about the first presiding bishop's tenure. "Prior to Haywood it (PAW) was predominantly white." Haywood's affiliation with PA W, however, brought in an' 'influx of Black brothers." His presence also helped the growth of PAW in the Midwest.

Until then most of the affiliated churches were located in the west "where it started."

Bishop Golder stated that the Pentecostal Assemblies of the World is also indebted to Bishop Haywood for its reorganizational structure. Governmental pressures were surfacing quite frequently, and there was a need to be registered as a church organization. Bishop Haywood's role in this effort was underscored in relocating the headquarters from Portland, Oregon to Indianapolis, where Haywood pastored.

Another contribution of Haywood's was changing "the PA W to a semi-episcopal form" of church organization. PAW also experienced international development under G. T. Haywood. Churches were established "in Africa, India, China, and Japan." This was done in the late 1920's, a truly remarkable feat for Black Apostolics at that time.

One of the most outstanding contributions of G. T. Haywood, one that greatly impacted and benefited Apostolics in and out of PAW, was his writings. Many of his writings have been preserved and duplicated. Thus, thousands who never saw or heard G. T. Haywood have been recipients of his marvelous God-given mind.

At the death of Bishop Haywood, the presiding bishopric went to a former foreign missionary, Bishop Samuel Grimes of New York.

The Grimes administration is remembered for several noteworthy achievements. As Bishop Golder reminds us, "He had the longest tenure as a presider (1931-1967)." Additionally, Bishop Grimes served as one of the very few non-pastoring bishops.

Most Apostolic bishops also pastor for three reasons. First, a good strong congregation provides the bishop with support for his issues and programs. Secondly, the apostolic organizations are not structured to support bishops outright; therefore, bishops receive monetary compensations from their local congregations. Thirdly, the tenuous structure of Apostolic church organizations would require a bishop to have faith of the highest magnitude to make it without pastoring. But in all fairness to Apostolic laity, many of the self-proclaimed bishops do not merit organizational support because of their lack of effectiveness as bishops.

However, Bishop Samuel Grimes went against tradition and served over 30 years as a non-pastoring bishop.

Obviously, a man of great organizing ability, Grimes successfully "set up thirteen (13) state councils, from Massachusetts to Florida, and presided over all of them. This particular ability was not just limited to the United States. In addition to churches in other foreign countries, the Grimes administration expanded to the' 'British West Indies and Leeward Islands."

The teaching ability of Bishop Grimes came to be legendary among Black Apostolics; and hundreds flocked to hear him at every opportunity. Bishop Samuel Grimes died in 1967.

Succeeding Bishop Grimes was Bishop Ross Paddock from Kalamazoo, Michigan. Paddock, who had served as the assistant presiding bishop to Grimes, became the first white to head PAW since it went to the bishopric system in 1925.

Speaking about Bishop Paddock's contributions to PAW as presiding bishop, Golder said, "Paddock is given credit for being an excellent presiding officer. (He) knew how to. guide a convention, whether stormy or calm." Golder added that Bishop Paddock kept a "cool head in turbulent times."

Rule -changes by PA W prevented Paddock from serving for life. With his assistant presider, Bishop Frank Bowdan, who was Black, Bishop Paddock concluded his administration in 1975. This marked another rarity for Apostolics. Seldom has a presiding bishop's tenure concluded without serious illness or death. Neither case applied to Bishop Paddock.

The year 1975 ushered in the third integrated team of top officers in PAW. Starting with the Grimes-Paddock and the Paddock-Bowdan teams, the team of Bishop Francis Smith (Black) and Bishop Lawrence Brisbin (white) took over.

Under the Smith Administration, PAW has made important strides. Probably the most important project to date has been the purchase of a shopping center that will be converted to the international headquarters. This facility will include a 7,500-seat worship center, the Aenon Bible College, and a publishing company. Projected date for at least a partial opening of the headquarters is 1982.

The Pentecostal Assemblies of the World, the mother of all Apostolic organizations, also continues to be one of the largest. A staff of over thirty (30) bishops serves 1,000 churches with a membership that is in excess of 450,000.

Apostolic Overcoming Holy Church of God, Inc.
1915

This church denomination was originally organized in 1915 as the Ethiopian Overcoming Holy Church of God by Bishop William Thomas Phillips. Prior to his Apostolic converting, Phillips was with the Methodist Church. His concern for a lifestyle of holiness spurred him to do independent study of the scriptures, which led to an independent revelation of Apostolic doctrine. There is no evidence that Bishop Phillips had prior contact with any known Apostolic leader or teacher; there was, however, subsequent contact with G. T. Haywood.

In 1927, Bishop Phillips changed the church name, replacing Ethiopian with the word Apostolic. According to church spokesperson Dorothy Roby, the name was changed to reflect the inclusion of white members, and to identify the church more clearly as an Apostolic denomination.

The administration of Bishop W. T. Phillips spanned 59 years. Under his leadership, the church denomination grew to 300 churches, from coast to coast, and in India, Africa, and the West Indies. The

Phillips administration also operated a printing press, purchased the headquarters church in Mobile, Alabama, and bought a senior citizens home in the late 1950's. Bishop William Thomas Phillips' long tenure closed out with his demise in 1974. Succeeding Phillips was Bishop Jasper C. Roby of Birmingham, Alabama. During Roby's tenure as presiding bishop, the Apostolic Overcoming Church has expanded missionary efforts into Haiti.

Other accomplishments include development of a second senior citizens home and a church-supported school. Headquarters have since moved to Birmingham, Alabama.

Church membership under the Jasper Roby administration now exceeds 125,000, a small percentage of which is white. Doctrinal positions support women in the ordained ministry and remarriage after divorce under some conditions. Assisting Bishop Roby is vice-bishop C. R. Harris and an executive board.

Church of Our Lord Jesus Christ of the Apostolic Faith, Inc.
1919

Within Black Apostolic circles, organizations are often referred to simply by their founder or presiding bishop's name. The Pentecostal Assemblies of the World has often been referred to as "Haywood & Grimes' work" and the Pentecostal Churches of the Apostolic Faith as "Hancock movement." One of the

Apostolic organizations that is known primarily because of the respect, popularity, and admiration accorded its founder is "Lawson's body." This simply means that one does not mention the Church of Our Lord Jesus Christ (COOLJC) without simultaneously thinking of Bishop R. C. Lawson, the founder and first presiding bishop. According to Mable L. Thomas:

> The life of Bishop R. C. Lawson is tantamount to the history of the Church of Our Lord Jesus Christ... for his life was built around the church.[10]

In the book, *For the Defense of the Gospel,* which is a compilation of biography and writings of the late Bishop Lawson, one learns of his early meeting with Bishop G. T. Haywood. During a severe illness that had been diagnosed as terminal, Lawson was carried to the Apostolic Faith Assembly. This church, in Indianapolis, was. pastored by Bishop G. T. Haywood. The following passage ~suggests what followed:

> Accepting the word of God, he (Lawson) was baptized in the name of the Lord Jesus Christ. He received the blessed baptism of the Holy Ghost and was healed and raised from a consumptive bed.

> Upon reception of the Holy Spirit, he became an ardent student of the Bible, following in the footsteps of his father in the gospel, G. T. Haywood.[11]

---

[10] Arthur M. Anderson, ed., *For the Defense of the Gospel* (New York: Church of Our Lord Jesus Christ Publishing Co., 1971), p. 6.
[11] Ibid., pp. 6-7.

This incident happened in 1913. Shortly thereafter, R. C. Lawson proceeded to establish churches in Texas, Missouri, and Columbus, Ohio. It was from the pastorate of the thriving church in Columbus that Lawson left for the East. He reached New York City on July 1, 1919. From a street corner preacher, then-Elder Lawson was invited to use the homes of the James Andersons and the James Burleighs. It was located at 56 East 131st Street. From this place a new Apostolic organization came into being, the Church of Our Lord Jesus Christ of the Apostolic Faith.

In addition to being a very eloquent and powerful speaker, Bishop Lawson was also a magnetic and charismatic personality. This was evidenced early in his New York ministry. Again and again, larger structures for worship had to be secured. While the New York church was growing, affiliated churches of the organization were also being established in other areas of the country. It was in 1923 that administrative structure was given to the Church of Our Lord Jesus Christ.

At that time, Bishop Karl Smith, who had succeeded Lawson at the Columbus, Ohio Church, accepted the position as executive secretary of the general church body. (Smith also, on another occasion, served in a similar capacity with the Pentecostal Assemblies. of the World. He eventually severed his relationship with Lawson and returned to PAW, where he distinguished himself in subsequent years by starting the Aenon Bible College. The school continues to serve as PAW's only educational institution, and one of the very few subsidized by a Black Apostolic church.)

6/3/2023

As COOLJC continued to grow and prosper, new programs were added. In the early 30's, Refuge Church (the mother church) initiated a broadcast ministry in the greater New York area. The response was measured by yet more people coming to join the Refuge Church of Our Lord Jesus Christ. This was, however, just one of the projects at Refuge that caused Bishop Lawson to become one of the all-time outstanding ministers produced by the Apostolic churches.

In the field of business, this man of God proved that he was not a novice. At a time when many Pentecostals and Apostolics were finding sin in everything, Lawson was organizing funeral homes in the large Black community of New York City. Many years prior to the present popularity of day care centers, Refuge had a day nursery. Additionally, Bishop Lawson owned a grocery store, a book store, record store, and a small publishing office. In the office, *The Contender for the Faith*, the official church organ, was published.

One of the stories that has been handed down about R.C. Lawson is that "the man was so 'heavy' that he went to bed with a book and woke up with a book. There was obviously some truth to the story, because Lawson admitted that he "read voraciously." Not only did Lawson read insatiably, he also provided encouragement and a means for aspiring ministers to do the same. One must remember that Bishop Lawson espoused and supported the need for a higher-trained clergy in the 1920' s.

This was a time when the vast majority of Black Apostolics felt that the Bible and the Holy Ghost were sufficient tools for the preaching of the gospel. Even today the fact is that a very few -Black Apostolic organizations require any minimal educational standards for their clergy. Consequently, the educational level among Apostolic ministers runs the spectrum from persons who have not finished elementary school to persons who have post-seminary training.

In the education of clergy, Lawson was a pioneer. He started the Church of Christ Bible Institute in 1926. After years of operation as a substandard, but very meaningful and helpful level, the school was fully accredited in 1950 by the Board of Regents of New York State. Dean James L Clark, Sr., one of the early religious educators in the Apostolic church, who by then had assumed tutelage, was very instrumental in the accreditation efforts.

While the Bible institute serves primarily adults, Lawson also saw the need for a school on the elementary and secondary levels. With that in mind, he established the R. C. Lawson Institute in Southern Pines, North Carolina. With J. J. Anderson as the principal, the school received its accreditation in North Carolina before 1945.

Bishop R. C. Lawson set a definite imprint on the Apostolic church, more specifically the Church of Our Lord Jesus Christ. Through his prolific writing ability, many of his ideals, concepts and interpretations are still read and followed today.

The growth of the mother church, Refuge, has been paralleled by the growth of the national church, *COOLJC*. In addition to the continuing development of congregations in various sectors of America, COOLJC began to take on an international character. Trips to the West Indies, the Virgin Isles, Antigua, Jamaica and

Trinidad, between the years 1935 and 1945 by Bishop Lawson resulted in the establishment of affiliated churches in those countries.

After twenty-six years, there were problems for the headquarters. The structure on West 133rd Street, New York City, with a seating capacity of 1,000 was becoming too small for the International Convention. As a matter of fact, the structure was generally overcrowded at the regular Sunday morning service. After looking and praying, the bishop decided to move his large contingent of followers:

> The Lord directed Bishop to purchase a magnificent building from the Lowe's Theatrical Corporation for $75,000...
>
> To our knowledge, this was the first time a Pentecostal church had purchased a theater in order to renovate it for the purpose of worshipping
>
> God. Many frowned on Bishop for purchasing a theater, calling it a Devil's house ... Shortly thereafter, however, many Pentecostal churches followed in his footsteps. [12]

The seating capacity for the new church was 3,500, more than tripling the capacity of the former structure.

When discussing the historical development of COOLJC under the able and competent administration of R. C. Lawson, the scripture in Proverbs 29:18 comes to mind:

---

[12] Ibid., pp. 12-13.

Where there is no vision, the people perish: but he that keepeth the law, happy is he. (KJV)

One would be hard pressed to deny the fact the Bishop Lawson had a vision. And contrary to that of many Apostolics, his was not local, or even regional in its scope. As the 20's marked his missionary journeys to Latin America and the Islands, the 40's produced several journeys to Africa. These missionary treks continued into the 50's. In 1958, the first convention of the Church of Our Lord Jesus Christ in West Africa was held.

All of this enormous growth abroad and at home did not occur with full cooperation. As a matter of fact, some persons had left COOLJC just as Bishop Lawson had left PAW. The reasons, however, were not necessarily the same. The fact remains that splits and schisms characterize the Black Apostolic denominations. One observes these statements relative to COOLJC:

It has been stated that any organization must suffer the pangs of growth, and the Church of Our Lord Jesus Christ was no exception. There have been several organizations and/or independent churches that have been an outgrowth of the ministry of Bishop Lawson, either directly or indirectly. Among them have been the Church of the Lord Jesus Christ, Bishop S. C. Johnson, founder. (Note proximity of names: Church of Our Lord-Lawson; and Church of The Lord-Johnson); The Way of the Cross Church, Bishop H. C. Brooks, founder. In the year 1957 there was a major schism within the ranks of our organization (COOLJC) when the Bible Way Churches of Our Lord Jesus

Christ World Wide was organized with Bishop Smallwood Williams, Presiding Bishop.[13]

Bishop S. C. Johnson split with Bishop Lawson over the mode of dress for female members. Bishop Brooks, however, desired to pastor his church independent of organizational affiliations. Bishop Smallwood Williams, on the other hand, disagreed with some of the administrative policies of Bishop Lawson. More will be said on these three gentlemen later. In addition to these three men who left and eventually headed their own organizations, at least two other ministers left COOLJC. They were Bishop Willie Giles and Bishop John Pernell.

In 1960, at the age of 77, Bishop Lawson made what became his last trip to Africa-Liberia. On that trip he witnessed the water baptism of twenty-eight persons. Of this total, twenty-four received the baptism of the Holy Ghost.

On June 30, 1961, the earthly life of this gifted orator, self-educated man, and pioneer Apostolic minister, R. C. Lawson, ended on a highly spiritual, cosmic level:

> The nurses who attended (Bishop Lawson) stated that he was delirious much of the time. In his delirium he was heard to say, 'I'm ready,' I'm baptized in Jesus' name and filled with the Holy Ghost;' 'Even so, come Lord Jesus.' Nurse Maude James related that during the last half hour, Bishop became quite calm. At approximately 10:20, he began to speak in tongues in a soft voice. He

---

[13] Ibid., p. 19.

continued until about 10:30, at which time he asked, 'Is the broadcast over?' Hearing the answer 'yes,' he said, 'Lord I'm ready; take my hand,' and Then he was gone.[14]

Bishop Hubert J. Spencer of Ohio was designated with the herculean task of succeeding Bishop Lawson as head of COOLJC. He had to follow a man who served as founder and presider of the church, for the entire forty-one years of its existence. Bishop Spencer, however, courageously accepted the mantel of leadership.

In an effort to get more information about the Spencer administration of COOLJC, Elder Wilbur Jones, editor of "Contender For The Faith," (the official publication of The Church of Our Lord Jesus Christ), was interviewed. He is also pastor of Beulah Church of God in Brooklyn, New York and a district elder.

The most important contribution of the late Bishop Hubert Spencer was his role as "a stabilizer." Jones said, "the years 61-63 were a (critical) transitional period (that) needed a father image." From all indications just as R. C. Lawson was the man to be the founding pioneer, Spencer's task, though not nearly as publicized, was just as important. For it was the stabilizing and conciliating influence of Bishop Spencer that helped to bring about a cohesive effect, thus keeping the organization together.

One must remember that Bishop Spencer assumed the presiding apostleship under two extremely heavy burdens. First of all, Spencer had to follow a legend, and

---

[14] Ibid., p. 22.

an institution, R. C. Lawson. Secondly, the Church of Our Lord Jesus Christ was still in the process of healing subsequent to the "big split" in 1957. Added to these two cumbersome burdens, was the fact Bishop Spencer also began losing good health.

Had a lesser person with inferior ability been in the presiding apostleship between the administrations of Lawson and Bonner, the results might have been catastrophic. The Church of Our Lord Jesus Christ could have split in many different groups. As the work continued, however, some splits did occur.

In addition to the three men who left and eventually headed their own organizations: (Bishops Johnson, Brooks and Williams) two others left. These two left after the founder's death. Bishop Willie H. Giles of Eden, North Carolina left because of continuous disagreements with his diocesan superior, Bishop John Pernell of Richmond, Virginia. And Bishop Pernell left COOLJC somewhat later because of some doctrinal differences.

Bishop Giles had been appointed overseer for parts of North Carolina, and pastor in Eden. His father, "Daddy" Giles served as the. assistant pastor. Giles' sisters and brothers were the controlling faction in the church. They were in turn supported by children, nieces and nephews. Bishop Giles' departure from COOLJC did not cause much of a national stir in the church.

On the other hand, Bishop John Pernell's exit caused considerable uproar. Prior to his leaving, Pernell had gone to a general convention with what he considered to be a new revelation. The only problem was that his revelation cut right at the heart of the Apostolic doctrine. Rather than emphasizing the name Jesus as the current dispensational name of God, Pernell argued that Yahweh, an Old Testament name of God, was the appropriate title for God in this church age. Being an Apostle in COOLJC meant that Pernell exerted an influence over other local congregations in addition to his own. This new interpretation was a serious problem because Bishop Pernell had gained respect as a Bible student in his own right.

The COOLJC Governing Board, concluded that Pernell's position was contrary to the teaching and doctrine of the church, and he was charged with being in error. Having apparently reached an irreconcilable state, Pernell pulled out and formed his own church body. The name included in part the *Assembly of Yahweh.*

Some felt that competition for the presiding apostleship was also a cause of Pernell's leaving. District Elder Wilbur Jones made the following comments: "Bishop Pernell was a noted scholar in the organization. (He) had probably given himself to as much study as any minister. His closest peer in scholarship was Bishop Henry Jones. "

Wilbur Jones added that "As it became increasingly apparent that Bishop William Bonner would succeed Bishop Spencer it seemed to present some problems for Bishop Pernell. "After all," Jones added, "Pernell was Bonner's senior."

Looking specifically at the more advertised reason for Bishop Pernell's leaving, everything revolved around the controversy of the name Yahweh as opposed to the name Jesus.

W. L. Bonner, in his book, *My Father In The Gospel*, says, "I think one of the things that hurt me so very much was when Bishop J. W. Pernell came up with a new doctrinal concept of the name, using the Hebrew Yahweh instead of the English name Jesus. We talked about that, but he was convinced that the Lord had shown him a new revelation, and he was determined to pursue it."

Bishop Bonner's subsequent comments really get to the heart and soul of the controversy.

> He told me that Jesus means nothing. I responded, you were healed... through the name Jesus, you were blessed... 30 years... through the name Jesus; and yet you are going to tell me that the name Jesus means nothing?[15]

At Bishop Hubert J. Spencer's death, he was succeeded by Bishop William Bonner, pastor of the headquarters church. This rise to the top position by Bonner fulfilled a bit of prophecy he experienced. Bishop Bonners' book, *My Father In The Gospel,* notes that for reasons unknown to Bonner, Bishop Lawson picked Maurice Hutner to be junior pastor and share in the limelight during opening of the Refuge Church at 124th Street and Seventh Avenue. Prior to this time, when the church was on 133rd Street, Bonner had been junior

---

[15] William L. Bonner, *My Father in the Gospel* (New York), p. 50.

pastor. In the words of Bishop Bonner, "I had served in the office of junior pastor as well as I had served as chauffer. There wasn't anything I had failed to do. Yet that day I felt I was cut off. I sat there looking at Bishop Lawson receive all of the honors from the VIPs (including late Congressman Adam Clayton Powell, Jr.) and Maurice Hutner carrying on as the junior pastor. I sat there, my heart almost bursting. But the Lord spoke to me and said, 'Do you see that seat Bishop Lawson is sitting in? I will give YOU that seat. Be patient.'"[16]

Patience and experience paid off. Years after the death of Bishop Lawson, Bishop William Bonner officially sat in the Presiding Apostle's chair.

Splits and setbacks notwithstanding, the Church of Our Lord Jesus Christ has continued to move forward under the leadership of Dr. William Bonner with tremendous and significant growth.

During one three-year period, forty-seven new churches were started. The Bonner administration has sought to put churches in every state in the union.

Two programs that W. L. Bonner has initiated and implemented are relatively new for Apostolics. The first is the development of a retirement plan. Few, if any, other apostolic organizations have any kind of a retirement plan. Secondly, COOLJC has begun sending ordained

---

[16] Ibid., p. 34.

elders into new areas and supporting them for six months. Heretofore, Apostolic ministers pioneered new churches without denominational assistance.

The Bonner administration has also been characterized by international development. Health clinics and churches have been established in Africa; and churches have been set up in Germany, England, and Trinidad.

Presiding apostle W. L. Bonner is assisted by regional apostles Henry D. Jones, Perry Thomas, J. P. Steadman, and Frank Solomon. They oversee the affairs of 450 churches with approximately 300,000 members.

The Original Glorious Church of God In Christ Apostolic Faith, Inc.,
1921

Another Black Apostolic organization, the Original Glorious Church of God in Christ Apostolic Faith, Inc., has historical roots dating back to 1921, although 1952 is usually set as its date of origin. Bishop I. W. Hamiter, the presiding bishop, provided enlightenment relative to the Glorious Church's history.

He stated, "The Glorious Church of God in Christ Apostolic was founded in 1921. Bishop C. H. Stokes got the incorporation and charter."

It was in 1928, however, that we hear of the man whose personal situation supposedly led to a major organizational problem, Bishop S. C. Bass. He became presiding officer of the Glorious Church of God In Christ in 1928. From that time until 1951, there were no significant problems involving Bishop Bass. However, in 1952, after the death of his first wife, S. C. Bass remarried. The problem arose because the second wife was a divorcee. According to Bishop I. W. Hamiter, "that was against church doctrine. For years we had been taught that it was wrong to marry a divorced person." The resulting effect was the standard Apostolic split. Hamiter says that "about 25 churches (out of a total of 50) left after Bishop Bass got married."

Bishop Hamiter was asked why the splinter group did not align with an existing Apostolic organization. He said there was "no particular reason for not going with an existing group; we just did not want to." One would also imagine that strong loyalty to a particular organizational name played a part. Often when a group of Apostolics have been identified by a certain name, they will fight before surrendering that name. The irony is that countless splits bring about a never-ending list of new names anyway.

In 1952, augmented by a goodly number of Glorious Church supporters, Bishop W. O. Howard started the Original Glorious Church of God in Christ, Apostolic Faith. The word ORIGINAL was added for two reasons. First it signified a break with those who still chose to follow the leadership of Bishop S. C. Bass. Secondly, according to Bishop Hamiter, the Howard group kept the charter that dates from 1921.

For the next twenty years (1952-1972), Bishop W. O. Howard served as presiding bishop of the Original Glorious Church, and only stepped Gown then because of poor health. During those twenty years the Howard administration made noteworthy achievements. First, as Bishop Hamiter put it, because of Howard's "stabilizing influence, he was able to keep the organization together."

The other primary accomplishment of the church achieved under the Howard administration was the addition of approximately fifteen more churches. The Original Glorious Church soon had about as many churches as had been affiliated prior to the 1952 split.

Closing the active W.O. Howard era in the Original Glorious Church did not stop the growth and development by any means. It merely laid a foundation for the I. W. Hamiter administration to build on. And build it did. From the forty churches that made up the organization at his inauguration, Bishop Hamiter has built the Original Glorious Church to a total of 165 churches (fifty-five in the continental U.S., and 110 on foreign soil). The other countries include Haiti, Jamaica and India.

Also, under Bishop Hamiter's leadership, the organizational body has completed the purchase of a convention center. This facility, in Columbus, Ohio, will serve to centralize many of the organizational activities in years to come.

It should be added that the convention center idea seems to be catching on among some Black Apostolic organizations. Several are in the process of developing similar projects. As Apostolics continue on this path, it may be helpful for some to talk with the Memphis-based Church of God in Christ. This church, the largest Black Pentecostal (though not Apostolic) church in the U.S., has had a convention temple for many years. There are, however, some who feel that going to Memphis every year, as opposed to taking the international convention to various cities, has handicapped the churches. It is felt that more people in more areas would become familiar with Church of God in Christ through the rotating convention system.

In the international structure of the Glorious Church of God In Christ, Apostolic Faith, Bishop Hamiter is assisted by Bishops. O.D. Fitzpatrick, David Blunt, and James Bell. James H. Smith carries the title of honorary bishop. Additionally, the organization has almost 300 ministers scattered throughout the 165 churches. According to Bishop Hamiter, total church membership is approaching 25,000.

Asked about the possibility of the two Glorious Churches getting back together, Hamiter replied, the "two groups have talked, but have never been able to bring it to pass." Hamiter added that since his group has far outgrown the Bass group (now presided over by Bishop Perry Lindsey) "they would have to concede." Essentially what that means is most of top positions would be retained by Hamiter and his group. No doubt Bishop I.W. Hamiter would serve as the presiding bishop of a reunited Glorious Church.

Way of the Cross Church of Christ
1927

Around 1926, Henry C. Brooks, a tall, handsome Black man from the Carolinas went to Washington, D.C. Brooks, who acknowledged that he had been "called to preach" sought to get the necessary credentials. According to his widow, Mrs. Willie S. Brooks, the bishop went to Bishop Lawson in New York to get a minister's credentials. He was told to first go back to Washington and work with Elder J. T. Morris (Highway Church) for a year. Brooks went back to Washington, but he did not serve under Morris. He started the first Way of The Cross Church of Christ in 1927. A second church was started shortly thereafter near Henderson, North Carolina. Within a short time, Brooks received his credentials from Lawson.

Elder Alphonzo Brooks, son of the late Bishop H. C. Brooks, said, "Daddy was with Bishop Lawson from 1928-1933. He left because Lawson wanted him to turn his church over to Bishop Smallwood Williams and work with him." Alphonzo Brooks added, "At that time both men (H. C. Brooks and S. E. Williams) had small congregations." For some reason "Bishop Lawson preferred one larger church in Washington, D.C. rather than two smaller ones." Rather than acquiesce to that arrangement, Brooks went independent. That independence remained until Brooks officially started the Way of the Cross Church organization.

According to Mother Willie S. Brooks, the widow of Bishop H. C. Brooks, her husband had no intentions of starting an organization. In fact, he was against it. But Alphonzo Brooks gave us some insight as to how it all happened. "Bishop Brooks only wanted to pastor his local church. He felt that there were no worthy benefits in an organization. The organization really got started because others came to him and wanted to work with him. He was finally encouraged to be the leader of several churches interested in working together. And that's really how Way of the Cross got started."

The Washington, D.C. pastorate of Bishop Henry Chauncey Brooks spanned forty years, 1927-1967. With a local membership of about 3,000 members, H. C. Brooks led the new organization in establishing churches up and down the eastern coast.

Bishop H. C. Brooks, who was known as the Supreme Bishop of the Way of the Cross Church of Christ, Inc., was succeeded by his brother-in-law, Bishop J. L. Brooks. The new bishop gave up his local church in North Carolina and moved to Washington, D.C. to become pastor of the headquarters church.

Even though development moved forward, Way of the Cross was not without schisms. Among those who left and became presiding bishops themselves were Bishop Ralph Green, Bishop Joseph H. Adams, and Bishop Joseph Weathers. Bishop Henry Williams also left. Rather significantly though, both Adams and Weathers left after C. Brooks died in 1967.

Alphonzo Brooks also said, "In the Black Apostolic church, many of the brethren get to a point where they feel a need to do their own thing without answering to anybody. That's when they usually leave." Many times, the desire to become a bishop, or a presiding bishop, is sufficient reason for leaving. If the present organization does not decide to elevate a person, then self-consecration is always an option.

Brooks said Bishop Joseph Adams left Way of the Cross to start United Way of the Cross because "He felt that the time had come for him to move on. Just as Lawson left the Pentecostal Assemblies of the World (PA W) and Daddy (H. C. Brooks) left Lawson, Adams felt it was time to leave too." One notes that Elder Richard Adams, the brother of Bishop Adams, chose not to leave Way of the Cross. And while their churches are twenty miles apart, they are in different Apostolic denominations.

Prior to Bishop Adams withdrawing from the Way of the Cross in 1974, Bishop Joseph Weathers (then Elder Weathers) left in 1969. Weathers leaving created a considerable uproar; especially at the headquarters church. Knowing that every controversy has two sides, this writer talked with Bishop Joseph Weathers and Elder Alphonzo Brooks about this unfortunate experience.

Weathers stated that he "should have been given consideration for the pastorate" of the headquarters church. Weathers mentioned his years of loyal dedication and support to Bishop H. C. Brooks and Way of the Cross. But Weathers was upset because "Alphonzo Brooks was not even preaching at the time of Bishop Brook's death in 1967." Weathers added that he felt that some at Way of the Cross Church were trying to keep the pulpit available until Alphonzo Brooks gained enough experience to become pastor. (Elder Alphonzo Brooks was appointed pastor of the headquarters church in 1978.)

Weathers concluded by saying, "If Alphonzo had been preaching at the time of Bishop H. C. Brooks' death, I would have supported him for the pastorate. But under the circumstances, I felt I had no choice but leave." The impact of Weathers' leaving was shown by the fact that over one hundred active members left with him and started a new church, the Holy Temple Church of Christ.

However, Elder Alphonzo Brooks stated, "Weathers' situation was different from Adams, Green, Williams, and Neal (other ministers who left the Way of the Cross).

Prior to Daddy's death, Bishop Weathers was pastoring churches in Ashland and Mineral, Virginia. Immediately after Daddy (H. C. Brooks) died he (Weathers) just stopped going to those two churches and came back to the headquarters."

What happened during the first year after Bishop H. C. Brooks' death was a novel experience for a Black Apostolic church. In essence, the Black Baptist church system of selecting a minister was adopted. Three ministers were used on a four-month rotational basis. They were Elders Willie Davis, Walter Thompson and Joseph Weathers. But, according to Elder A. Brooks, "At the end of Weathers' four-month term, he did not want to leave."

This system was abolished after a year, and Bishop John L. Brooks assumed the pastorate of the headquarters church. J. L. Brooks moved to Washington, D.C. from Henderson, North Carolina in 1969, and stayed until his retirement from pastoring in 1978.

One certainly has to marvel at the stamina and leadership ability of Bishop John Brooks. Very few ministers would have dared move from a relatively tranquil comm unity like Henderson to Washington, D. C., especially if they were past seventy years old. At his retirement from pastoring, J. L. Brooks was 82. Bishop John L. Brooks, continues to serve as the presiding bishop of the Way of the Cross Church of Christ.

Looking at the national church under the administration of J. L. Brooks, two achievements stand out. First, is the proliferation of bishops. From three between 1927 -196 7, Way of the Cross consecrated twelve bishops between 1968-1979. The second hallmark of the J. L. Brooks administration is the international development of the Way of the Cross Church. The year 1979 marked the addition of thirteen churches and missions in Ghana and Liberia, West Africa.

Presently the Way of the Cross organization has 48 affiliated churches and a membership of approximately 50,000 people. In addition to Bishop J. L Brooks, church officers include: H. C. Eggleston, vice-bishop, and Bishops J. H. Hicks, Myles Meredith, S. B. Davis, N. L. Bridges, L. H. Cannady, J. A. Green, R. B. Fuller, W. M. Jackson, C. W. Hairston, J. E. Williams, and Moses Achempong.

Highway Christian Church of Christ
1929

The Highway Church had its beginning in Washington, D. C. James Thomas Morris, who had been an elder with the Pentecostal Assemblies of the World, founded this denomination in 1929. The new church organization was chartered in 1939. Morris, who later moved to New York to pastor, "was ordained bishop in the year of 1941 by Bishop J. M. Turpin."[17] Here again we see a direct link to the first Apostolic organization through Bishop Turpin.

One of the accomplishments of the Morris administration was the establishment of several affiliated churches. Bishop Morris died April 23, 1959 and was succeeded by his nephew J. V. Lomax. Bishop Lomax, who had formerly been a member of Refuge Temple under R. C. Lawson, is given credit for one achievement as presiding bishop. According to spokesperson, Minister Herman Jinwright, "many people have received the Holy Ghost during revivals conducted by Bishop Lomax."

Highway Christian Church has been labeled one of the more conservative organizations listed as Apostolic. Part of its belief is that dressing should consist primarily of black and white. Therefore, men wear black suits, white shirts and black ties. Women wear white dresses, or white blouses and black skirts.

---

[17] Carrie Wheeler, ed., *The Path of Life Through Highway Christian Church of Christ, 1968.*

Pastels and other bright colors are considered loud, flashy, ostentatious, and therefore worldly.

As for women ministers, the Highway Church will accept a woman who is already ordained, but this organization will not ordain women. Further, if a woman pastor desires to affiliate with Highway Church, she must relinquish her pastorate to a man.

The total membership of all thirteen affiliated churches is 3,000. Serving with Bishop J. V. Lomax on the board of bishops are Samuel Redden, vice-bishop; and Bishops Divens, S. Hunt, and A. E. Carr.

Church of the Lord Jesus Christ of the Apostolic Faith

1930

This Philadelphia-based church group was started by Sherrod C. Johnson. Johnson had been a state overseer with the Church of Our Lord Jesus Christ under the leadership of R. C. Lawson. The local church that Johnson pastored in Lawson's organization was started in 1919. When a split occurred between Bishops Lawson and Johnson in the early 1930's, Johnson's local church also defected and became headquarters for the new denomination, whose name changed only one word "our" to "the" in its title.

Johnson and Lawson disagreed over the mode of dress for female members. While Lawson was not opposed to females wearing jewelry and makeup, Johnson was. Women in Johnson's church must wear cotton stockings, calf length dresses, unstraightened hair, and head coverings. Other doctrinal beliefs include non-observance of traditional Christian holidays (Christmas, Easter, and Lent).

In Apostolic denominational circles, Bishop S. C. Johnson was known as ultra-conservative and as a fierce exponent of the doctrine. At the death of S. C. Johnson (1961), Apostle S. McDowell Shelton succeeded him. Under Shelton's leadership,' the church continues to publish its monthly periodical, *The Whole Truth,* and broadcast a syndicated radio program. Additionally, the Church of the Lord Jesus owns an ultra-modern headquarters building and an adjoining garden apartment complex. Together these structures are labeled Apostolic Square.

Bishop Shelton is one of the most widely travelled prelates in the apostolic churches, having made ceremonial trips to visit with more than a dozen heads-of-state.

A difference in this church hierarchical structure from other Apostolic groups is seen in its national officers. Laypersons dominate these positions, heading seven of the nine posts in the national church. In most Apostolic groups, clergy lead the various auxiliaries.

The Church of the Lord Jesus Christ has 100 churches in the United States, England, Africa, Jamaica, and the Bahamas. Membership estimates have ranged from 5,000 to 5 million.

The Apostle Church of Christ in God
1940

The Apostle Church of Christ in God grew out of a split from the Church of God (Apostolic). According to J. C. Richardson, Sr., the split occurred because of a difference concerning administrative procedures with Bishop Eli Neal.

Bishop Thomas Cox was still listed as the presiding bishop of the Church of God (Apostolic), but poor health had resulted in his being inactive. Bishop Eli Neal was serving as state bishop and acting presiding bishop.

Neal was reluctant to get input from other ministers and ran an operation that was pretty much a one-man show. There was also concern about personal problems that Neal was experiencing. And, as is the case with far too many Apostolic groups, the differences were resolved by schism.

Some consideration was given to connecting with an already existing Apostolic church body. However, those who were planning to leave felt that starting a new organization was better for essentially one reason. Having been affiliated with only a regional body, the Church of God (Apostolic), the splinter-group ministers realized that they were not that familiar with other Apostolic denominations. While the Church of God (Apostolic) had its strongest appeal in the Southeast, most of the other Apostolic groups at that time were concentrated in the North and Midwest.

Thus, in 1940, a group of five ministers decided to start a new Apostolic organization that would be headquartered in Winston-Salem, North Carolina.

In the year 1940, Elders J. C. Richardson, J. W. Audrey, Jerome Jenkins, W. R. Bryant, and J. M. Williams were impressed by God to establish an unshakable structure as his ambassadors for the rehabilitation of falling humanity and as contenders for the faith. It was located (headquartered) at 5 ½ Greenwood Avenue, Winston-Salem, North Carolina. They organized this great work known as the Apostle Church of Christ in God. [18]

At the time, this church was organized, it had three affiliated churches. They were the St. Paul Apostle Church, Rudd, North Carolina; J. W. Ardrey, pastor; Mt. Sinai Apostle Church, Martinsville, Virginia; J. C. Richardson, pastor; and the Bethlehem Apostle Church, Winston-Salem, North Carolina; J. M. Williams, pastor. From the original five organizers, J. W. Ardrey was elected to be the first presiding bishop. Shortly thereafter, the original five added another minister, Elder Walter J. Jackson, who had been with Bishop Faison.

---

[18] James C. Richardson, ed., *Apostle Church of Christ in God Discipline*, p. 2.

Gradually, the new church began to establish itself and grow. With growth the need became obvious for another bishop. Therefore, at the 1952 General Assembly in Newport News, Virginia, Elder James C. Richardson, Sr., was elected to be the second bishop.

The new organization was little more than thirteen years old when the possibility of a split developed. Elder Robert O. Doub, by then state overseer of Pennsylvania, had vehemently expressed his personal displeasure that Bishop Ardrey was the presiding bishop. According to Doub, Ardrey lacked the ability and competence to lead the ACCG effectively. The board did not support Doub, but kept Ardrey as the presiding bishop because growth had been realized under Bishop Ardrey's leadership. (The organization by then had churches in New York, Pennsylvania, as well as other sections of Virginia and North Carolina.)

Elder Doub, however, would not compromise or reconsider his position. Thus, with his local congregation as a base of operation, Doub founded and incorporated the Church body, Shiloh Apostolic Temple, Inc., in Philadelphia, Pennsylvania. Only about two or three other churches from the Apostle Church of Christ in God went with Doub. But the "split" syndrome had nonetheless manifested itself among the ranks of the new church organization.

Subsequent events gave a measure of support to Bishop Doub's position. About a year after Doub's departure, Bishop Ardrey did in fact step aside as presiding bishop. The man whom Doub had supported against Ardrey, Bishop J. C. Richardson, became the new presiding bishop of the Apostle Church of Christ in God in 1956.

Under the leadership of Bishop Richardson, ACCG has achieved its highest level of success. This South Carolina native began an intensive program of church development. By this time, his local congregation had grown to the point that he could be supported without additional employment. He was thus free to do much of the detailed work involved in setting up new congregations. Concentrating his efforts primarily in Virginia and the Carolinas, Richardson either organized or assisted other ministers in organizing ten churches. He personally pastored at least three of them; his present pastorate (in Martinsville, Virginia.) included. Feeling that the organization was not yet able to retain legal counsel, Richardson personally paid lawyers in every state in which the ACCG operated so that local churches could be registered and certified as non-profit, tax-exempt organizations.

Two other noteworthy achievements were initiated under the administration of Bishop Richardson. The first was the institution of an official publication. Originally called *The Apostolic Gazette,* the name was changed to the *Apostolic Journal.* This bi-monthly publication enjoyed a rather fruitful existence before it was discontinued. The second project was the birth of the Educational Fund. This fund was started to assist members from affiliated churches who continued their educational training beyond the secondary level. In 1961, at the age of fifty-one, this successful pastor and bishop entered seminary to get additional training himself.

For three and one-half years, three days a week, Bishop Richardson drove one hundred and eighty miles to and from seminary. He did this while maintaining his pastorate and position as presiding bishop. That kind of determination provided an incentive and motivation for many of the other bishops, elders, and ministers, as well as laity.

Just when it seemed that the Apostle Church of Christ in God was making real progress, another minister defected. Around 1962, Elder George Wiley of Yonkers, New York decided that his qualifications equipped him for the office of bishop. Furthermore, he expressed this to the official board. However, the board refused his request, and Elder Wiley left the Apostle Church of Christ in God. He has since formed his own organization and serves as its presiding bishop. Sister Lucille Wiley had served as president of the General Youth Department and Elder Wiley had been quite popular in the organization. Therefore, many wondered if others would leave and join the new bishop, Bishop Wiley. Such was not the case. In fact, Wiley's brother (Elder Joseph Wiley) refused to leave ACCG. A warm spirit of fellowship continues to be shown between the two groups.

The church recovered from this split and continued on its mission. Several congregations joined with the Apostle Church of Christ in God. As the 60's drew to an end, ACCG seemed on the brink of moving from a regional to a national church in character. Some mergers had been discussed, and a few possibilities seemed feasible. Many felt that the 1970 General Assembly had been the best organized and the most unified. But people had barely finished reflecting and rejoicing before disaster struck.

True, there had been two relatively small splits, but 1971 was the year of THE SPLIT! That year the Apostle Church of Christ in God was torn right down the middle. Years of hard work for many persons was snatched away as if someone had abruptly pulled a giant rug from under ACCG. The pains and hurt were most severe.

The reasons for the split have not clearly been articulated. Many hidden agendas, however, began to surface in the form of personality attacks based on old feuds and envy.

With few exceptions, the ministers who left have remained together as a new church denomination with Bishop Ardrey.

Although there are deep regrets about the split that took place in 1971, the churches that make up the organization have pulled together, and done a good job. According to Bishop J. C. Richardson, "the programs presented in the councils, assemblies and jubilees (since 1971) have been the best since the Apostle Church of Christ in God has been organized." Richardson said, "The programs are now more educational, diverse and more interesting." Various seminars, lectures and workshops have been added. An example is Convention Bible School for the younger children.

In terms of exposure, experience, and educational development, ACCG has moved forward in the last ten years. Though the numerical growth does not match the level prior to the split, finances exceed amounts collected when there were twice as many churches.

As far as ministers leaving, Bishop C. R. Washington of High Point, N. C. and Elder Joseph Wiley of Goldsboro, N. C. were two to leave since the departure of Bishop Tilman Carmichael in 1974. C. R. Washington left after losing a lawsuit to retain control of the church he pastored. Joseph Wiley left because of a desire to be his own bishop. There has been speculation that Wiley is interested in starting his own organization.

One must note that Elder (now Bishop) Joseph Wiley chose not to join his brother, Bishop G. H. Wiley who is General Overseer of the Mount Hebron Apostolic Temple of Our Lord Jesus Christ. G. H. Wiley, who left ACCG some years ago, maintains his headquarters in Yonkers, New York. As far as Bishop C. R. Washington, to date he has maintained an independent status with the new congregation that he started.

With many apostolic organizations, especially the relatively smaller ones, growth does not come through the establishment of new churches, but through accepting already-existing congregations. They may be independent churches or congregations that have been with apostolic denominations. In this regard, ACCG is no different from other apostolic groups.

Since 1971, growth in ACCG has come by adding established groups. Ministers who have joined during this time include Bishop Jeremiah Jefferson and Bishop E. Cartledge in the Washington, D. C. metropolitan area; Bishop C. L. White, Winston-Salem, N. C.; Pastor Arenn Wynn, Youngstown, Ohio; Elders Harry Betts, South Boston, Virginia; James Benton and Benjamin Joyner, North Carolina; Ashley Brown, Washington, D. C.; and James Brooks, United States Air Force chaplain. Additionally, Elder Roosevelt Watson resigned as pastor of the Zebulon, North Carolina church to start a new group in Winston-Salem. And the significance of that is Watson's church is the only completely new home mission effort started in the ACCG in the last ten years.

It is remarkable when one considers that many Apostolic ministers like J. C. Richardson, Sr., and W. J. Jackson (vice-bishop of ACCG) have labored over 38 years with one group, knowing that a split at any time could negate all their efforts.

Looking at the general church, the Apostle Church of Christ in God, has five bishops, twenty-five ministers, thirteen churches, and 2,150 members.

Shiloh Apostolic Temple, Inc.
1953

In the never-ending proliferation of Apostolic organizations, Shiloh Apostolic Temple, Inc. must also be added to the list. From an affiliated congregation of the Apostle Church of Christ in God, Shiloh developed into yet another organization after becoming independent in 1953.

In August 1948, Robert O. Doub, Jr. left Winston-Salem, North Carolina for the "city of brotherly love" to organize a new congregation. In addition to developing the congregation in Philadelphia, Doub was also active as an evangelist trying to start churches in other areas. It was Dou b' s efforts in home mission development that eventually led to his leaving the Apostle Church of Christ in God.

According to Bishop Doub, "I was working up churches in the state (Pennsylvania), and another person (Overseer Melvin L. Jones of New York) was getting credit. I asked to be made a bishop over my churches, but Jones was against it." Bishop Doub concluded by saying he felt that he was totally justified in his request.

Added to his feeling of being over-worked without recognition or adequate appreciation, was what Doub perceived as poor leadership by Bishop J. W. Audrey who was then presiding bishop of the Apostle Church of Christ in God. In the opinion of Doub, Audrey lacked the ability, vision and motivation to be a presiding bishop. These two reasons became the basis for the Shiloh Temple in Philadelphia becoming headquarters for another organization.

Shiloh's organizational status did not take effect immediately. Efforts were made to align with the Church of God in Christ (Apostolic) headquartered in Baltimore, Maryland. Bishop Randolph Carr was the presiding bishop. Bishop Doub stated, "Carr and I had worked out most of the details for me to go in with them. But there was one problem. Bishop Monroe Saunders, who was the number two man in the organization, didn't seem to want me in. I don't know what the reason was, but it didn't work out."

After leaving the ACCG and feeling somewhat rebuffed by some Church of God in Christ (Apostolic) officials, Doub (at the tender young age of thirty) set out to start his own organization. From the time of incorporation with only one church in 1954, Shiloh Apostolic Temple has grown to twenty-three churches. Eight are in England, and two are in Trinidad.

Starting with the headquarters church of 500 members, Shiloh Apostolic Temple has two other bishops, thirty minsters and a total membership of 4,500. Accomplishments under the administration of Dr. Robert O. Doub, include publication of an official organ, *Shiloh Gospel Wave;* the opening of Shiloh Promised Land Camp in Montrose, Pennsylvania, and expansion into an international church. Since the inception and development of Shiloh, it too has experienced its share of ministers joining and leaving.

Pentecostal Churches of Apostolic Faith
1957
This church organization was co-founded by one of the Black Apostolic pioneers. Along with Elder David Collins, Bishops Heardie Leaston, and Willie Lee, Bishop

Samuel Hancock was extremely instrumental in starting this group. Prior to PCAF's origination in 1957, Samuel N. Hancock had served as one of the initial seven bishops of the Pentecostal Assemblies of the World.

Bishop R. L. Little, the general secretary, has said that Bishop Hancock' 'formed another organization because of a desire to maintain a high standard of holiness." According to R. L. Little, Bishop Hancock felt that the standard had been lowered in the Pentecostal Assemblies of the World (PAW), and "was being jeopardized." Bishop Little did acknowledge, however, that S. N. Hancock taught that Jesus was only the son of God, and did not teach the traditional Apostolic doctrine that Jesus is God.

From the birth of the organization on October 24, 1957, Bishop Hancock served as presider until his demise in 1963. Bishop Willie Lee served until 1964. Then problems arose. Bishop Lee served as presider of a splinter group; while a group headed by Bishop Elzie Young kept the PCAF charter and the chartered name.

Bishop Willie Lee and his followers also taught that Jesus was not the one God, but only the son of God. However, the majority sided with Bishop Elzie Young and were strong proponents of the original oneness doctrine.

The irony of all this is that the Young and Lee factions split over the Godhead issue. Bishop Lee's teachings were similar to Hancock's. Although the Young-led group tolerated Bishop Hancock's deviation from the Apostolic doctrine, Bishop Lee's was not accepted. From 1964 to the present, Elzie Young has been the presiding bishop of the Pentecostal Churches of Apostolic Faith.

The accomplishments of PCAF under the Young administration have proved to be quite impressive. First of all, the PCAF financial structure is strong, since all of the churches contribute a percentage to the national treasury. Secondly, PCAF's "foreign mission work has increased. Missionaries are being totally supported by the church." Bishop Little, who is the overseer for foreign missions, talked with considerable pride about this area. He remarked, "It took a while to get many of the members sold on this (foreign missions), but now it is doing quite well."

Under the supervision of Bishop Little, the foreign mission budget has gone from an annual $3,000 to $40,000. Efforts abroad are concentrated in Haiti and Liberia, West Africa, where a school has been built.

The Pentecostal Churches of Apostolic Faith have 115 churches, 380 ministers, and a total church membership of approximately 25,000. Bishop Elzie Young, the presider, is assisted by Bishops D. Rayford Bell, Lewis B. Stallworth, Alfred Singleton, J. O. Franklin, Robert L. Pullen, A. J. Walker, and R. L. Little.

Bible Way Church of Our Lord Jesus Christ World Wide
1957

Many people tend to think that the Bible Way organization is one of the oldest Apostolic churches in existence. Such is not the case. The *Bible Way Church of Our Lord Jesus Christ World Wide, Inc.,* was born out of a National Pentecostal Ministerial Conference, September 25-29, 1957 in Washington, D. C. It was held by Drs. Smallwood E. Williams, John S. Beane, McKinley Williams, Winfield Showell, James I. Clark, and Elder Joseph Moore, some of whom were former officers of the *Church of Our Lord Jesus Christ of the Apostolic Faith* (Lawson).

> This conference was called to consider some mal-administrative practices, which we were convinced were out of line with New Testament collective leadership as practiced by the Apostles, and authoritarianism, which we could no longer tolerate. From this Conference, five ministers were consecrated Bishops, namely: S. E. Williams, John S. Beane, McKinley Williams, Winfield A. Showell, and Joseph Moore.[19]

At this service of consecration and birth of another Black Apostolic organization, Bishop John S. Holly, an officer of the Pentecostal Assemblies of the World, officiated. However, as early as 1927, Bishop Smallwood E. Williams had come to Washington, D. C. at the request of Bishop R. C. Lawson. His purpose was to establish and build a church. Williams, who was at that time affiliated with the Church of Our Lord Jesus Christ, named his Washington church the Bible Way Church of Our Lord Jesus Christ. For thirty years Williams and Lawson maintained

---

[19] 20 Smallwood E. Williams, ed., *Official Directory of the Bible Way Church of Our Lord Jesus Christ World Wide, Inc.* (Washington, DC: Bible Way Press, 1962), p. 9.

affiliation. For about twenty-five of those years, Lawson functioned as presiding bishop, with Williams functioning as the general secretary. There was a close and harmonious relationship between the two men. Many wondered why the split occurred. Bishop Smallwood E.

Williams alluded to "mal-administrative practices" in the Church of Our Lord Jesus Christ. In further elaboration, Bishop Williams said:

> I had no disagreements with Bishop Lawson's doctrine. It was very sound. But he (Lawson) would not consider making anybody else a bishop. And there were many men in the organization who were qualified for the position.

> He (Lawson) acted like a dictator and wouldn't change, so we left. You see, I believe in collective leadership. The New Testament tells of twelve apostles, not just one.

Bishop Williams maintains that his position must have had some justification because of Bishop Lawson's subsequent actions.

> He (Lawson) proved that we were right, because not long after we left, Bishop Lawson began to 'make other bishops.

As a result of this administrative difference, Bible 'Way Church of Our Lord Jesus Christ, which had only been a local congregation affiliated with Lawson's group, became, in 1957, an incorporated church denomination. (The local church in Washington, D. C. had preceded the organization of the Bible Way denomination by some thirty years.)

In the Bible Way News Voice, the official church paper, (July-August, 1958) Bishop Williams listed ten mistakes of Lawson relative to the split. Among them were these two:

> It was a mistake for him (Lawson) to attack others as promoting themselves when he did exactly that himself, when he pulled or split out of the Pentecostal Assemblies of the World about the year of 1919, and set up his own movement, inviting others to join him.

> It was a mistake for him to promote himself to the exclusive class of the only bona fide Apostolic Faith Bishop, as long as he lives, none other.[20] [21]

The accusations in this article did not go unchallenged. Bishop Lawson responded to Williams' article with his own:

> It is claimed that I promoted myself to the exclusive class of the only bona fide Apostolic Faith bishop as long as I lived, and none other. This is a lie, and Elder Williams knows it. His memory seems to be long on some things, but may I call his memory back to the time when I appointed state bishops to the Church of Our Lord Jesus Christ. This is how Bishop S. C. Johnson got to call himself a bishop. When I saw the pride and wrong

---

[20] S. E. Williams, "Bishop Lawson's Mistakes Viewed," *The Bible Way News Voice,* Vol. 5, No. 2 (July-August, 1958), p. 5.

impression people were taking as bishops, I merely changed it to State Overseer... No one demurred... This thing is a conspiracy by Elder Williams to take over the church, and sub plant me on the grounds that I was getting too old. This is pride in one's self as being young, hence more capable.[21]

Since the split, the COOLJC and BWWW have both continued to function and progress with their respective leaders. What is more important, some fellowship now takes place between the two organizations.

Whatever disagreements one might have with Bishop Smallwood E. Williams, he must be given credit for his accomplishments and contributions to the Black Apostolic church. He has distinguished himself as a brilliant administrator and competent pastor. He has also been one of the few Apostolic ministers who has consistently spoken out about the social problems in our society. Bishop Williams' ministry is just as other-worldly as most Apostolics. But his interest in politics, housing, jobs, and the like, shows a concern for the total needs of the people. This dimension of social ministry is extremely conspicuous by its absence among the majority of Apostolic ministers. Under Williams' leadership, the Washington Bible Way Church has sponsored the construction of a large apartment complex. A supermarket is also sponsored near the apartment. For years, Bishop Williams has not been reluctant to speak out on politicians and vital political issues. In his book, *Significant Sermons*, many

---

[21] Anderson,, *op. cit.,* p. 266.

of the twenty sermons are addressed to contemporary social issues.

While he has been busy preparing the people for the "hereafter," Bishop Williams has also been busy helping conditions in the "here and now."

One of the first five bishops of the BWWW denomination was Winfield Showell of Baltimore, Maryland. Showell's church is very important historically. In this pastorate, Showell succeeded his uncle, J. M. Turpin, one of the seven initial bishops of the Pentecostal Assemblies of the World. The First Apostolic Church then is one of the oldest congregations under the Apostolic church - banner. And two of the leading Apostolic ministers have served it as pastors. In the twenty-three years that BWWW has been an organization, there have been no major splits within the ranks. When one considers the fact that Bible Way 81 started with seventy churches in 1957 and now has 300 churches and missions, with approximately 250,000 members, one sees an enviable growth record among Black Apostolics.

"We have not had a split because of the dynamics of the leadership," claims Bishop Lawrence G. Campbell of Virginia. The ability of Bishop Williams to preside and his charisma are both vital assets. Additionally, Campbell believes geography of membership is important in the prevention of schisms. "The BWWW churches are heavily concentrated on the East Coast." Since all of the top bishops live in the East, "they are close to the ministers and churches. Contact is easy, and there is a spill-over of influence."

Speaking more specifically about the dynamics of leadership in the Bible Way organization, Campbell stresses the contribution of the initial bishop board. The diversity of personalities that came together under one banner has been a source of strength for the BWWW organization.

Looking first at Bishop Smallwood E. Williams, the presiding bishop, Campbell makes these statements:

"Bishop Williams has emphasized education. Not only has he maintained a Bible school at the headquarters church for many years, but he has also supported a school in Africa."

Bishop Williams has also been involved with social and political issues and affairs. This has helped to give Bible Way an image of total concern about its members and others."

Steady growth of the general church is due to a moderate doctrinal stance (by S. E. Williams). and the national organization's willingness to help individual churches. Added to that, Smallwood Williams has been a flexible and progressive leader. In fact, at the age of 72 he is involved in leading the Washington congregation in its fourth building program.

Balancing S. E. Williams' moderate position is "the martinet or strict disciplinarian" co-vice bishop McKinley Williams. The mixture has obviously worked quite well for Bible Way. Indeed, what has emerged for the BWWW constituency is a synthesized doctrinal position. However, the fundamental tenets of Apostolic doctrine are unchanged.

Supplementing these two contributors is former Pentecostal Assemblies of the World (PAW) minister, Bishop Winfield Showell. An interesting thing about Showell and Smallwood Williams staying together so long is the issue of women in the ordained ministry. While Williams has been opposed to women preachers, Showell's position was obviously nurtured by the Haywood-Grimes teaching in favor of women ministers. This issue has torn asunder many Apostolic groups, but it has not had a major negative effect on the Williams-Showell relationship or on the BWWW organization.

Further comments by Campbell: in regard to Dr. Showell provide some helpful insights as to why harmony and unity have prevailed. "Bishop Showell is a pastor's friend. He is also a conciliator, he brings people together, heals wounds and bridges the gaps."

In addition to these three bishops who continue to play very significant roles in the leadership of Bible Way Church, three others contributed greatly to the birth and development of the Bible Way Church of Our Lord Jesus Christ World Wide. They included Bishop John S. Beane, who served as the first vice-presiding bishop until his death. According to Bishop Campbell, Dr. Beane's most significant contribution to Bible Way was his gift of healing. Time and time again the Lord used Bishop Beane as His instrument to touch and or raise up some individual who felt at the end of the road.

Another sturdy, valiant and resolute member of the initial board of bishops of Bible Way was Bishop Joseph Moore of New York. According to Campbell, Moore was a man dedicated to fasting and prayer. It was not unusual at all for Bishop Moore to go on a 21-day shut-in fasting and praying. Further accentuating the spirituality of the man was his humility and patience.

Rounding out this second ecclesiastical triumvirate was the Rev. Dr. James I. Clark, Sr. Perhaps more than any Black Apostolic minister of his generation, Dr. Clark epitomized education. Not only had Clark been successful in getting state accreditation for R. C. Lawson's Church of Christ Bible Institute, but he brought the same kind of zeal to the Bible Way denomination. In years to come, should the Lord delay His return, Dean James I. Clark, Sr., will long be remembered for his pioneering efforts in education. Men such as J. I. Clark, Sr., and R. C. Lawson, along with G. T. Haywood, S. Grimes and K. F. Smith emphasized the importance of education as a part of preparation. However, in 1980, far too many Black Apostolic ministers earnestly seek inspiration while vigorously avoiding education in their efforts for preparation for the Gospel ministry.

Of the first six bishops, only Bishops S. E. Williams, McKinley Williams, and Winfield Showell are still living. Since McKinley Williams is blind, if Smallwood Williams decides to retire as presiding bishop, obviously Showell would become the second presiding bishop of Bible Way.

Further down the road, speculation centers on either Bishops Huie Rogers of Lawrence G. Campbell becoming chief prelate. Both men are comparatively young (late 40's-early' 50's), dynamic preachers, conscientious pastors, and competent administrators. It is probably too early to make a prediction as to which is in the favored position, for both are inordinately popular and influential in the national church.

Since much of Bible Way church history is rooted in the Church of Our Lord Jesus Christ (COOLJC), some ask about the possibility of the two groups merging. Campbell replied, "I don't see it happening because no one wants to give up his position of power." Bishop Campbell added, "I don't see the sense of it, (all Black Apostolics in one organization). I don't think oneness has to be one organization, but one doctrine."

The Bible Way Pentecostal Apostle Church
1960
Just as the Black Apostolic movement has large organizations with affiliates throughout the continental United States and foreign countries, so too does it include small groups that operate within one state. The Bible Way Pentecostal Apostle Church falls under the latter heading. In fact, all four of the affiliated churches are within a ninety-mile radius. This denomination has national officers, all in the state of Virginia.

A look at its roots shows that the founding presiding bishop formerly held membership in two other Apostolic organizations. Bishop Curtis P. Jones, the founding bishop, began his ministerial career under the aegis and pastorate of Bishop Eli Neal. Based in Winston-Salem, N. C., Neal was then serving as a state bishop in the Church of God (Apostolic).

From Winston-Salem, Jones was sent to Roanoke, Virginia to establish a church. This took place in 1933. Some five years later, then Elder Curtis Jones became disenchanted with the leadership of Presiding Bishop T. J. Cox and split from the Church of God (Apostolic). Opting at that time to go with a larger, well established group, Jones aligned himself with the Church of Our Lord Jesus Christ of the Apostolic Faith. (Bishop R. C. Lawson was the presiding bishop.)

It was also about this same time that C. P. Jones became pastor of the St. Paul Apostolic Church in the Axton community of Henry County, Virginia. A Reverend Sister Phanelson was the founding pastor of this church. Although C. P. Jones and Sister Phanelson had worked together in past years, Jones' alignment with R. C. Lawson signaled a repudiation of women ministers, since Lawson was vehemently opposed to females serving as ordained ministers.

About the time of the great split in the Church of Our Lord Jesus Christ in 1957, C. P. Jones decided to make another move. Initially, he indicated intent to join the Bible Way Church of Our Lord Jesus Christ. Although

Jones left Lawson, he did not go with Smallwood Williams, but decided to form his own organization.

In 1960, with churches in Roanoke, Henry County, and Franklin County, Virginia, Jones started the Bible Way Pentecostal Apostle Church. While C. P. Jones pastored the Roanoke church, he turned over pastoring responsibilities to Elder Edward Martin at the Henry County Church in Axton. Martin had been a member of the Axton St. Paul Apostolic Church. Another former St. Paul member, Elder Aaron Moyer, started a new mission in Franklin County, near Rocky Mount, Virginia, the Gethsemane Church-of Christ.

Bishop C. P. Jones served as presiding bishop until his death in 1976. Some assumed at that time that Edward Martin, who was general elder, would become presiding bishop. After all, he was the next man in line. Further, there were only four churches, so competition was thought to be minimal. However, opposition to Martin was so strong and fierce, that he was effectively blocked from becoming the new presiding bishop.

This action had a disappointing effect on Martin. He later declared himself a bishop, but the Bible Way Pentecostal Apostle Church still refuses to accept him as its presiding bishop. He is, in actuality, only bishop of his local congregation. So, Martin is with the organization, and yet he is not with the organization. He continues to fellowship with the other churches and elders, but there is opposition to Bishop Edward Martin becoming general presiding bishop. Discussions are taking place in an effort to resolve the differences. Both Bishop Martin and Elder

Aaron Moyer indicate that a reconciliation appears imminent and possible.

True Vine Pentecostal Churches of Jesus, 1961

This Black Apostolic organization, founded and presided over by Dr. Robert L. Hairston, has a very interesting history. Prior to becoming Apostolic, Hairston had been associated with Trinitarian Pentecostals. In fact, he served as co-founder and vice-bishop of the True Vine Pentecostal Holiness Church along with the late Bishop William Monroe Johnson. (At Johnson's death, his son Sylvester D. Johnson, became pastor of the Winston-Salem, N. C. headquarters church and presiding bishop of the True Vine Pentecostal Holiness Church).

For more than twenty-five years, Hairston had a ministry with several Trinitarian Pentecostal Church groups. But in 1961, Rev. R. L. Hairston accepted baptism in Jesus' name. This happened because he became convinced that it was biblically correct. "After having talked with several of the Apostolic people as well as my older sister, who was already Apostolic, I became convinced that Jesus name baptism was right." Unlike many Apostolics who thought that salvation cannot occur without water baptism in Jesus' name, R. L. Hairston "had no doubts about being saved prior to getting baptized in Jesus' name."

Interestingly enough, it was not Bishop Hairston's refutation of the trinity doctrine that led to his departure from the True Vine Pentecostal Holiness

Church. The split came about because of church policy differences between Johnson and Hairston, as well as Hairston's marital problems.

In regard to general church policy, Dr. Hairston felt that convocation assessments were too burdensome for smaller churches. Bishop W. M. Johnson, who pastored one of the larger churches, insisted on the higher fees. Of course, the presiding bishop was not to be denied or repeatedly challenged in this church nor in most Black Pentecostal or Apostolic churches. Hairston, also a very strong-willed person, decided that Johnson's policies were unfair, So with his growing congregation in Martinsville backing him, Hairston left the Trinitarians.

Many say that it was really the marital problems that led to Hairston's departure from Johnson's True Vine Pentecostal Holiness Church. In late 1960, Bishop Hairston and his first wife separated. After several conferences with Johnson, R. 1. Hairston and Mrs. Sallie D. Hairston decided reconciliation was not possible and divorced. Bishop Hairston has since remarried Mrs. Gertrude Tarpley Hairston.

During the ordeal of his separation and divorce, R. L. Hairston expressed disillusionment with the lack of Apostolic support. It was not so much that Hairston sought approval from his Black Apostolic brothers, but rather understanding. According to Hairston, he "expected a closer fellowship with the Apostolics than with Trinitarian Pentecostals. Such has not been the case. Hairston added, "some who condemned my divorce have condoned similar actions by their own members."

As for his local congregation, leaving the Trinitarian Pentecostal Church and his divorce have had minimal effect. "The church has experienced its greatest period of growth since becoming Apostolic." One who is familiar with this congregation has to admire the unity displayed in spite of the extensive adversity the church has endured.

R. L. Hairston said he formed a new church denomination' 'because of concern for the continuation of the church after my death." The charter would prevent any person or group from stepping in uninvited and taking over. Additionally, the True Vine Pentecostal Churches of Jesus was formed because some members were reluctant to join other existing Apostolic organizations for "fear of running into similar problems that had been experienced in the previous church organization."

Bishop Hairston's churches have formed their own organization, but they have made efforts to work with other groups.

In the early 1970's, Bishop Hairston and Bishop Willie Giles of Eden, N. c., temporarily formed 'an organizational fellowship. Each church group retained its own charter and organizational structure.

Soon divisiveness occurred over women preachers. Giles, who had been affiliated with Bishop R. C. Lawson, did not support them. (After all, this was one of the issues that caused Lawson to leave the original contemporary Apostolic church in 1919, the Pentecostal Assemblies of the World.) On the other hand, Bishop Hairston has always supported women in the ordained ministry. Because of an inability to adequately resolve this issue, Hairston and Giles went their separate ways.

The True Vine Pentecostal Churches of Jesus has experienced growth lately as a result of a chance meeting between Bishop Thomas C. Williams and Bishop Hairston in 1976 at a funeral of a mutual acquaintance. After some extensive conversation, Bishop Williams decided to attend the 1976 convocation of the True Vine Pentecostal Churches of Jesus.

R. L. Hairston and T. C. Williams then merged their separate organizations into one group. Bishop Williams became senior bishop and Bishop Hairston became presiding bishop. At present, this organization has ten churches and missions, two bishops, fourteen ministers, and nine hundred members. The largest congregation is the headquarters church, New Bethel Apostolic in Martinsville, Virginia.

Major accomplishments under Bishop Hairston's administration include "church expansion, confusion-free convocations, a general church newsletter, and a tremendous increase in free-will giving." One must also add to this list of accomplishments, the outstanding music department. Anchored by the New Bethel Church choir and musicians, the True Vine Pentecostal Churches of Jesus boasts one of the leading convention choirs among Apostolics.

Mount Hebron Apostolic Temple of Our Lord Jesus of the Apostolic Faith, Inc.
1963

A local church called Mount Hebron was started in Yonkers, New York in 1957, as an affiliate of the Apostle Church of Christ in God. In 1963, Bishop George H. Wiley, III, founding pastor of the Yonkers church, left ACCG, and incorporated Mount Hebron as another denomination.

Bishop Wiley said he felt a need "to build a vision the Lord gave me." He also said, he wanted "better outreach with young people across this nation."

Since becoming his own bishop, he feels that he has better utilized such outreach opportunities. "1 have been able to visit twenty states and set up a radio broadcast in the states of New York, North Carolina, and South Carolina." G. H. Wiley said his outreach efforts have caused Jews, Puerto Ricans, Blacks, and whites to get baptized in Jesus' name. This work "could not have been done as freely in another organization."

Other accomplishments of the Mount Hebron churches include: a Bible school in each local church and plans for senior citizens and children's' homes. Another project that Bishop Wiley started is an interdenominational Youth forum designed to get the input of young people in church programs, planning and implementation.

The Mount Hebron organization is composed of ten churches, fifteen ministers, and a total membership of 3,000. Assisting Bishop Wiley are Bishop E. Everett and Bishop William Jackson.

The United Church of Jesus Christ (Apostolic)
1965

The United Church of Jesus Christ (Apostolic) came into being as an incorporated church in 1965. Prior to this time practically all of the churches were affiliated with the Church of God in Christ (Apostolic), Baltimore, Maryland.

The latter organization was headed by Bishop Randolph Carr, who in 1945 left the Pentecostal Assemblies of the World to start his own organization. Since existing Apostolic organizations had fairly well saturated the mid-East, mid-West, and far West, Carr concentrated his efforts on the East, and outside the continental United States. As a result of these efforts, the Church of God in Christ (Apostolic) developed more than sixty churches in England, Canada, and West Indies.

In his teaching, Carr was rather precise in his interpretations on divorce and remarriage. Some of his subsequent actions, however, were totally contradictory to his teachings. The result was that many of his ministers felt that they could not support Bishop Carr. One of those who had serious questions about the situation was Bishop Monroe Saunders. This minister held dual positions as pastor of the Washington church and chief assistant to Bishop Carr, as general secretary.

Saunders was asked by Carr to leave. In reaction, nearly the whole organization defected from Carr. It was felt, however, that because the Church of God in Christ (Apostolic) had been organized by Carr, a name change would be feasible. This was done in 1965. Under the new name, First United Church of Jesus Christ (Apostolic), Bishop Saunders became the first presiding bishop.

Monroe Saunders is one of the very few Black Apostolic presiding bishops who has finished a fully accredited seminary and post-graduate studies. And the United Church of Jesus Christ has made commendable progress with his leadership.

As a church denomination, much emphasis has been put on education of clergy and laity. On a comparative basis, this organization probably has one of the highest percentages of trained ministers. Naturally, Saunders is a meaningful example. Also, the Baltimore headquarters church has moved to a new and larger edifice, along with the Institute of Biblical Studies, a church-supported and church-operated institution. According to Bishop Saunders,

> In the United Church, we emphasize the concept of each local, autonomous assembly maintaining an atmosphere that is conducive to constantly having the presence of the power of the Holy Spirit.

This is certainly in keeping with the Apostolic tradition of a spirit filled witness.

The United Church is also beginning to focus on the total needs of its parishioners. *The Center for a More Abundant Life,* in Baltimore, has various programs to address the diverse needs of the people. In addition to a very beautiful church edifice, the center has a unit for senior citizens. A full program of involvement will serve and assist persons residing at the senior citizens' complex. The center also has a large Community Social Service Department. This section also treats alcoholics and drug addicts. There is also a baby clinic and day care center. Finally, there is a counseling and referral service. Like Bishop R. C. Lawson some years ago, M. R. Saunders, too, appears to have a vision.

In the United Church there is an effort to do more with the church money. The tithes, Saunders contends, should be used to support the minister. But additionally, many local congregations support a working layman's group. These people, many of them full-time, will assist the pastor in training the laity to minister to the community.

Although there is more construction to be done at the Center for a More Abundant Life, the Creative Learning Center has already opened grades K-6, with the secondary school scheduled to start in the near future. These are used by the international church even though they are housed in Baltimore, Maryland at the headquarters.

Churches of this denomination in England engage in significant outreach efforts. "They are working with Third World Ministers of the Apostolic faith and with an ecumenical group on the race problem." Also, in England, Dr. Saunders has done lectures at the University of Birmingham, and was scheduled for a year's assignment with the renowned Pentecostal scholar, Dr. Walter Hollenweger.

In other areas of foreign development, the United Church of Jesus Christ has extended missionary efforts into Mexico, Trinidad-Tobago, Jamaica, and other parts of the Caribbean. Bishop W. Glaxciola, an independent Apostolic pastor in Mexico City, has begun fellowshipping with the United Church. Elder Robert Johnson, the general secretary, says formal affiliation is expected to occur soon.

To avoid splits, Bishop Saunders said, "We keep all doors open. Churches that make application to fellowship with us are free to leave anytime they choose." Saunders added, "No one has to leave angry, but can come and leave in a spirit of love. Of course, the churches that we have planted present no problem." Citing another denominational strength, Bishop Saunders stated, "We openly and freely discuss doctrine, finances, and any other areas of the church; this has made a difference."

While no major splits have occurred, ministers and churches have left the United Church. These include. Bishop George Owens and Bishop Murray from Boston, Massachusetts. Bishop Frank Saunders (Monroe Saunders' brother) is also rumored to have left the organization.

The United Church of Jesus Christ has 52 churches, 150 ministers, and a total membership of 75,000. Bishop Saunders is assisted in overseeing the church by Vice-Bishop Sidney Dunn, and Bishops Obediah Colander, Collie Lorick and Charlie Burroughs.

The Apostolic Church of Christ, Inc.
1969

On May 12, 1969, Bishop Johnnie Draft and Elder Wallace Snow co-founded the Apostolic Church of Christ, Inc., with headquarters in Winston-Salem, North Carolina. This organization was the off-spring of another Apostolic group headquartered in Winston-Salem, the Church of God (Apostolic).

Prior to May, 1969, Bishop Johnnie Draft had served as pastor of the Saint Peter's Church, the headquarters for the Church of God (Apostolic). He had also been an overseer in this denomination for many years. Not only did he separate from the organization, he also gave up the pastorate of Saint Peter's Church. Bishop Draft never publicly stated his reasons for leaving. He did say, "The Spirit of the Lord brought to me to start my own organization." He added that he gained considerable evangelistic and church development experience with his former church. Draft had served as overseer at different times over the states of Pennsylvania, Virginia, North Carolina, and South Carolina.

The possibility of reconciliation with The Church of God (Apostolic) is not probable. Draft stated, "I don't foresee it taking place. I don't know what's in the future, but I don't foresee it at this point."

Accomplishments under Bishop Draft's administration include the purchase of the headquarters church (pastored by Draft), addition of new churches, building of an affiliated church structure in Mullins, South Carolina, and buying a church in Hampton, Virginia. To avoid defections, this church group has all local churches deeded to the parent body. Final decisions do not rest with the local group, but with the executive board.

There are six churches, one bishop, fifteen ministers, and 300 members.

The Apostolic Assemblies of Christ, Inc.
1970
The Apostolic Assemblies of Christ directly traces its roots to the mother organization of Apostolics, the Pentecostal Assemblies of the World.

Ten years ago, Bishop G. M. Boone, the presiding bishop, and others decided to form a new organization. Many of these had formerly been associated with the Pentecostal Churches of the Apostolic Faith, co-founded by the late Bishop Samuel N. Hancock from Detroit.

When Bishop Hancock died, "Bishop Willie Lee of Indianapolis, Indiana, became presiding bishop." Lee pastored the historic Christ Temple Church, which was at one time pastored by Bishop Garfield Thomas Haywood. During Lee's pastorate, Christ Temple left the Pentecostal Assemblies of the World and went with the Pentecostal Churches of the Apostolic Faith.

Bishop Lee served as presiding bishop from 1963-1968, but during the latter part of his administration, problems developed. "Questions arose," stated Bishop G. M. Boone, "about the Church charter. Bishop Lee had the charter but lost it, and others got it." Before the matter could be resolved, Bishop Lee died. Things were really left in shambles, and they did what Apostolics tend to do; they split into different groups. It was then that the tradition-rich Christ Temple Church left the Pentecostal Church of the Apostolic Faith and returned to PAW. (The church formerly pastored by Bishop Hancock also left. Under the leadership of Bishop Collins, this church has gone with the True Church of Jesus organization.)

Then a number of churches sided with Bishop G. M. Boone to form the Apostolic Assemblies of Christ, with Bishops Virgil Oats as vice-bishop, Willie Duncan as general secretary, and Fred Majors as treasurer.

Bishop Boone says, "The churches are growing, experiencing tremendous spiritual growth." Future plans include building a school.

Bishop Boone said that "every church is totally independent." No doubt this autonomy is suitable for most of the pastors, but it does not encourage corporate support for centralized projects.

The Apostolic Assemblies of Christ has six bishops, between 60-70 ministers, twenty-three churches, and a total membership of close to 3,500 people.

United Churches of Jesus, Apostolic
1970

As can be seen with so many other Apostolic organizations, the United Churches of Jesus Apostolic, was also born as the result of a split. This time the division occurred within the ranks of the Apostle Church of Christ in God. Many of the leading officials of the United Churches of Jesus, Apostolic (organized in 1970) had previously held top positions in the ACCG.

Bishop James R. Ziglar, who serves as vice general bishop, said there were two reasons for leaving the Apostle Church of Christ in God. The first reason was the fact that the Presiding Bishop of the Apostle Church of Christ in God, Dr. J. C. Richardson, Sr., had married a divorced woman. Secondly, there was a misunderstanding between the ministers.

The first reason dates back to November, 1970, when J. C. Richardson, Sr. met with the executive board of the Apostle Church of Christ in God, seeking advice on his proposed marriage to a divorcee. This meeting took place at the Mount Zion Church in Callands, Virginia. (Mount Zion, under the pastorship of Bishop R. B. Fuller, also pulled out, but joined the Way of the Cross Church rather than going with the United Churches of Jesus.) Although the current *Discipline* of the church does not forbid such marriages, Richardson voluntarily brought up the issue to see if there were any personal disagreements. (Local members of several churches included divorcees.) Dr. Richardson offered two alternatives: either he would marry the divorced woman and step down as presiding bishop, or not marry her and remain presiding bishop.

With the exception of Bishop Walter J. Jackson of Winston-Salem, North Carolina, all the ministers gave their unqualified support to Bishop Richardson and endorsed the marriage. Ironically, Bishop Jackson did not leave the Apostle Church of Christ in God, although many of those who said they supported the presiding bishop did leave.

Ironically also, a bishop who was twice-divorced (both former wives were still living) was accepted into the United Churches of Jesus Christ and placed on the executive board. After the split, fellowship between the UCJA and ACCG ceased. But some of the churches now participate in annual fellowship services together.

Bishop Ziglar said a new church denomination was started rather than affiliating with an existing Apostolic organization because "the older ministers wanted to set their own policies rather than going in under an already existing group."

Bishop Ziglar feels that the major accomplishments of the United Church of Jesus, Apostolic, are "the youth department, one of the most productive groups." Ziglar also added, "we give ten percent of everything raised to charity." Primary beneficiaries are college-bound high school graduates. Each year members of this group are presented monetary gifts to subsidize their educational expenses.

Bishop Ziglar said the church anticipates "starting a class to train new ministers to assist them in preparing for the pastorate."

The United Church of Jesus, Apostolic, has six bishops, thirty ministers, twenty churches, and approximately 2,000 members. Officers are: Bishop J. W. Ardrey, general bishop; J. R. Ziglar, vice-general bishop; S. W. Saunders, general secretary; U. I. McCall, -and Ernest Hairston, board bishops.

United Way of the Cross Churches
of Christ of the Apostolic Faith, Inc.,
1974

If the similarity in name of this church to another strikes you as familiar, it is for good reason. Prior to founding this church denomination, Bishop Joseph H. Adams had been with the Way of the Cross Church of Christ. In fact, Adams was serving on the board of bishops as a diocesan bishop over the state of North Carolina, when he decided to make his departure. Leaving the Way of the Cross Church of Christ, Bishop Adams, with the assistance of Elder Harrison J. Twyman, founded the United Way of the Cross Church of Christ in 1974.

Although this new organization did not commence operating until 1974, Bishop Adams considered the move as early as 1969. The split (or "resignation" as Adams prefers to say) was effectuated for a couple of reasons.

First of all, Bishop Joseph Adams disagreed with various administrative practices of the Way of the Cross Church. One must remember that at the time of the split, the founding bishop of the Way of the Cross, H. C. Brooks had died (1967), and Bishop J. L. Brooks (H. C. Brooks' brother-in-law) had become the presiding bishop. The disagreement was with Bishop J. L. Brooks; however, there are no ill feelings now and fellowship is taking place between the two groups.

Bishop Adams was invited to WOCCOC headquarters in Washington, D. C. to speak during Founder's Week, 1980. This is evidence that a spirit of fellowship exists between the Way of the Cross Church and the United Way of the Cross Church. (Bishop J. L. Brooks had by then retired as pastor of the Washington church. It is now pastored by Elder Alphonzo Brooks, son of the late Bishop Henry C. Brooks).

Bishop Adams also left the Way of the Cross Church of Christ after a vision. According to Adams, "Elder Harrison Twyman and I realized that God had given us similar visions to form a church organization." It would appear, then, that even if no disagreements had developed with the Way of the Cross Church administration, Adams was bound to leave because of the vision from God.

(Elder Twyman, the co-founder, had been affiliated with the Bible Way Church World Wide, and pastored in Madison, North Carolina. Twyman has since moved to Greensboro, North Carolina, where he now pastors).

Bishop Preston Graves is first vice-bishop of the general church. Prior to affiliating with United Way of the Cross, Graves had also been associated with the Bible Way organization.

Elder James Pickard, another board member and pastor, formerly held membership in the Apostle Church of Christ in God as well as other Apostolic organizations. Elder Pickard recently retired from pastoring in Reidsville, North Carolina.

There is also a very young bishop and pastor serving on the United Way of the Cross Church executive board and as chairman of the program committee. This person is Bishop S. David Neal of Seat Pleasant, Maryland. It is unusual for a minister to reach the bishopric at the young age that Neal did.

The youthful prelate was formerly associated with the Way of the Cross Church of Christ. He had, in fact, grown up in the Washington church. According to a Way of the Cross Church representative, Neal campaigned for the office of bishop prior to the 1978 annual convention. Although Neal felt that he had enough support to be elevated, opposition surfaced from one Neal considered a friend. Elder Alphonzo Brooks was among those highly vocal against Neal. The subsequent effect was twofold. First, Alphonzo Brooks and Neal terminated a close personal relationship; and secondly, Neal left the Way of the Cross organization.

The United Way of the Cross churches have four bishops, thirty ministers, fourteen churches, and approximately 1,100 members. Like most of the smaller Apostolic groups, United Way of the Cross is a regional organization, operating in five or six states.

Redeemed Assembly of Jesus Christ, Apostolic
1979

Not only did Bishop Edgar Butler split with Highway Christian Church and go with another organization, but two other ministers have left more recently and started another organization, the Redeemed Assembly of Jesus Christ, Apostolic, in 1979. The two ministers are Bishops James Frank Harris of Richmond, Virginia and Douglas Williams of Washington, D. C. These two men had been with the Highway Church in excess of twenty years, and both were relatively young (early 40's).

According to Harris, "we left because the church was controlled by one man, Bishop J. V. Lomax." Harris, Williams and other opposers also felt that Lomax had ceased providing vibrant and effective leadership. Bishop Harris added, "The Highway Church organization is stagnant." It was felt that new ideals were not accepted by Bishop Lomax.

> I.F. Harris believes that this kind of problem develops from the tradition than authority being vested in the executive board of the general church, most of the authority was given to the local church trustees in Washington. The general church executive board was originally set up to oversee church affairs, doctrinal and policy decisions, but Bishop Lomax actually

made decisions in conjunction with the local trustee board of Highway Church in Washington, D. C. Even though the Highway Christian Church of Christ has affiliated churches from New York to Florida, one local church determined policy for all. Further alienating Harris and Williams was the fact that the Washington church trustee board is primarily made up of laypersons, while the general church executive board is all clergy.

The Redeemed Assembly of Jesus Christ, Apostolic, started as a new group with six churches. However, only three of the churches were affiliated with the Highway Christian Church of Christ. Of the six, one is in Richmond, one is in New York, and four are in the Washington, D. C. metropolitan area (including suburban Virginia and Maryland).

The Redeemed Assembly of Jesus Christ is administered by an executive council and an executive board. The council consists of Harris and Williams, who are the presiding bishop and assistant presiding bishop, respectively. The executive board consists of the two bishops plus all other pastors.

Harris said they "started a new church denomination because of a vision that we desired to fulfill." Harris and Williams also wanted Apostolic leadership that did not emphasize denominationalism. According to Bishop Harris, "The majority of the Apostolic organizations have become engulfed in their own organizations."

Harris does not believe that organizations are a spiritual necessity. "Organizations are for convenience so that you can comply with the law of the land. It is a legal necessity rather than a spiritual necessity."

Chapter III

THIS WE BELIEVE

Historical Synopsis on Baptism of the Spirit

Practically all Black Apostolic organizations attempt to trace their origins back to A.D. 33, the Day of Pentecost. More important than the historical basis of the day, is the doctrinal emphasis given it. Just as 1906 A.D. marks the beginning of the modern Pentecostal Apostolic movement, it is believed that A.D. 33 ushered in the very first Pentecostal movement. The scriptural passage used to confirm the latter-day movement is the second chapter of Acts. This account is the first group meeting where people experienced speaking in tongues.

There are, however, at least two other scriptural passages in Acts that Apostolics use to give additional support for speaking in tongues. These passages are Acts 10:44-48 and Acts 19:1-7. It is acknowledged that there are no accounts of tongues-speaking in either the synoptic gospels, except Mark 16:17. In Paul's epistle to the Romans, no account of speaking in tongues is found either. It is only in Paul's first epistle to the church at Corinth that more information on tongue-speaking is given.

Paul's approach to glossolalia in I Corinthians 12-14 seems to be somewhat different than the accounts involving Peter in Acts 2:4 and Acts 10:44-48. As a matter of fact, there seems to be some difference in Paul's own attitude in Acts 19: 1- 7 compared to his Corinthian attitude. (Later in this chapter, an Apostolic understanding and interpretation of these accounts will be stated.)

After Corinthians, one finds no further information on either this *gift* or this *evidence* of speaking in tongues. Biblical history closes with no further documentation on the importance or use of speaking in tongues.

To the knowledge of this writer, there is no specific body of literature that traces a direct line of Pentecostalism from A.D. 33 in Jerusalem to 1960 A.D. at the Azusa Street Mission in Los Angeles. Thus, it is the intent here only to cite examples of groups within the designated time period (100 A.D. to 1900 A.D.) that might have had a Pentecostal "flavor" about them. Let it be noted, however, that by using the word "flavor," it should not be construed to mean that these groups were just emotional in worship. At least some in these groups actually experienced speaking in tongues. Obviously though, glossolalists did not receive the positive response prior to 1900 which they have received since.

In his book, *What Meaneth This,* Carl Brumback feels that adequate data can be found to show traces of perpetual usage of glossolalia as a spiritual gift.

In the second and third centuries, Brumback says, two persons, Irenaeus and Tertullian, were associated with glossolalia. Moving to the fourth century, one notes Pachomius and Augustine. About the latter, Brumback writes this:

> Augustine (354-430) wrote: 'We still do what the apostles did when they laid hands on the Samaritans and called down the Holy Spirit on them by the laying on of hands. It is expected that converts should speak with new tongues.[1]

From the fifth century to the Reformation, Brumback says, the gift of tongues was almost forgotten. Only the Waldenses and Albigenses are specifically mentioned by Brumback as speaking in tongues.

In the Reformation to post-Reformation era, Brumback mentions Martin Luther, Francis Xavier, and Thomas Walsh. Additionally, John Wesley did not condemn this gift; although there is no statement that Wesley experienced tongues.

Concluding the pre-twentieth century era, Brumback reminds us that the Quakers experienced speaking in tongues. He also relates a story about Dwight L. Moody. Rev. R. Boyd, who was a close friend of Moody's writes this about him:

> When I (a Y.M.C.A. member) got to the room of the Young Men's Christian Association (Victoria Hall, London), I found the meeting 'on fire.' The young men

---

[1] Carl Brumback, *What Meaneth This?* (Springfield, Missouri: Gospel Publishing House, 1947), p. 91.

were speaking with tongues, prophesying. What on earth did it mean? Only that Moody had been addressing them that afternoon.[2]

This Moody-led movement, eventually captured a good deal of support in London and surrounding areas.

Brumback, who is Pentecostal, feels that ample evidence exists in history to support belief that the gift was visible in all ages since 100 A.D.

On the other hand, Anthony Hoekema, who is non-Pentecostal, feels that a scarcity of information on the matter de-emphasizes the importance of the gift. In his book, *What About Tongue Speaking,* he does mention some people who apparently experienced glossolalia prior to 1900. Hoekema contends, however, that the rarity of this occurrence suggests that speaking in tongues is not so important. Regarding Montanus, the author has this to say:

> Pentecostal writers sometimes refer to Montanism as a movement in the ancient church, second century which is akin to their own...

> If, however, Montanism be cited as a precedent for Pentecostalism, it is a rather unhappy precedent, since the church judged Montanism's teachings to be heretical. ... Though it cannot be denied that tongue-speaking occurred among the Montanists ... this group hardly constitutes a strong recommendation.[3]

---

[2] Ibid., pp. 93-94.
[33] Anthony Hoekema, *What About Tongues Speaking?* (Grand Rapids, Mich.: Wm. B. Eerdmans Publ. Co., 1966), pp. 11-12.

After listing Irenaeus, Tertullian, Chrysostom and Augustine, saying that the gift did not appear in their day, Hoekema comes to the Middle Ages. Mentioning George Barton Cutten here, the author says:

> George Barton Cutten's *Speaking with Tongues* is hailed by students of the subject as the most thorough older history of tongue-speaking in the English language. His comments about the relative absence of glossolalia during the Middle Ages is quite interesting: 'It is rather surprising ... that in this age of wonders (the medieval period) it (the gift of tongues) appeared so infrequently.[4]

Hoekema does mention groups such as the Shakers, early Mormons, in addition to some early Methodists. But his overriding point is summed up in these words:

> The comparative silence of these many centuries of history as regards glossolalia ought to give serious pause to those who claim that the gift of tongues is one of the permanent gifts of the Spirit to the church.[5]

In addition to Brumback and Hoekema, other authors have attempted to understand the existence of tongues in church history. Watson Mills, in *Understanding Speaking in Tongues*, writes about the Cevennes in France. William J. Samar, in *Tongues of Men and Angels*, states that Edward Irving and Irvingites experienced glossolalia in the 1830's. And in *Tongues As of Fire*, Prudenico

---

[4] Ibid., p. 18
[5] Ibid., p. 23.

Damboriena writes about Cathars and the fact that they believed in a spiritual baptism.

In seems that what appears historically regarding glossolalia is scattered. Therefore, when one looks at the relatively few incidents of speaking in tongues from 100 A.D. to 1900 A.D., compared to the thousands since 1900 A.D., it raises a question. Why has there been such a long silence in terms of this particular gift being expressed? How does one make sense out of the fact that for 1,800 years only a few thousand people had the experience? But in the last seventy-five years, millions have experienced speaking in tongues.

The question cannot be adequately answered. Those against speaking in tongues have used this historical silence to support their claim. But such denial does little to explain the phenomenon from 1906 to the present. This present era of church history also has to be considered.

On the other hand, those who support speaking in tongues argue that there was official church suppression. During much of the silent 1,800 years under Roman Catholic domination, concerted efforts were made to keep such spiritual expressions out of the church. Hoekema presents another reason:

> Pentecostals counter that the reason this gift virtually disappeared from the church is that during these centuries (100 A.D. - 1900 A.D.), God's people were sinning against God, Christians failed to believe fully in all the promises of God, and the love of many waxed cold.

This position, however, presents problems for Hoekema, primarily for one reason. As he puts it:

> The difficulty with this interpretation ... is that it constitutes a wholesale indictment against 1,800 years of church history. Must we honestly believe that no Christians of past ages ... had the kind of faith, love and dedication shown by Pentecostal believers today? Was the entire history of the church from A.D. 100 to 1900 a history of apostasy?[6]

Without referring to the silent years as apostasy, at least one Black Apostolic organization offers an audacious explanatory statement which highlights the importance Apostolics put on speaking in tongues. The group is the Church of the Lord Jesus Christ of the Apostolic Faith, headquartered in Philadelphia, Pennsylvania. The late Bishop Sherrod C. Johnson was the founder (Bishop McDowell Shelton serves as the current General Overseer).

The statement is found in a leaflet entitled' 'The New Birth," distributed by this church organization. It reads:

> ... We will admit that after the death of the apostles, blindness prevailed upon the people for more than fifteen hundred years. In the time of this darkness and ignorance of God's truth, many prepared ways of their own, but thank God, in these last and evil days we can say that the darkness is past and the true light now shineth.

---

[6] Ibid., pp. 23-24.

And if one continues to read the leaflet, this "true light" is made clear.

> ... if you have not been baptized in water in Jesus Christ's name and filled with the Holy Ghost speaking with other tongues ... you are not saved; you do not have the New Birth Jesus spoke of.

Thus. what one has here is one Apostolic position on the explanation of the silent years. Other Apostolics may hold a similar rationale.

Historical Background: Baptism of Water

While some Pentecostal groups give less emphasis to water baptism so that the spirit might receive priority, such is not the case with Apostolics. It is common belief that unless one has been baptized in water in Jesus's name, the believer has not received all that he needs. One may ask if water baptism in Jesus' name (as opposed to the Trinitarian formula) preceded twentieth century usage?

It is helpful to begin with the biblical age. It is generally agreed that St. John practiced a baptism of sorts. His baptism was with (or in) water unto repentance. There was, however, a subsequent water baptism that was performed in Jesus' name. The first biblical account is found in Acts 2:32-41. At the urging of Apostle Peter some three thousand people were baptized in Jesus' name.

The book of Acts also lists other occurrences when baptism was administered, each time in the name of Jesus Christ. References to note here are: Acts 8:12-16, 10:48, and 19:5. There are also references to water baptism in Jesus' name in some of the epistles. More about this will be said later.

If it may be concluded that water baptism is biblically sound, should there not be some hint of a formula in the Bible? If so, does baptism in Jesus' name appear to be scripturally more correct than the trinitarian formula? The answer is yes. But it may help to give some attention to the traditional trinitarian formula.

Trinitarian baptizers have attempted to use the Bible to validate their formula. The scripture that readily comes to mind is St. Matthew 28:16-20. This scripture is commonly referred to (at least by Apostolics) as "The Great Commission." Keying specifically on verse 19, it reads:

> Go therefore and make disciples of all nations, baptizing them in the name of the Father, and of the Son and of the Holy Spirit ... (RSV)

This symbolic rite and ritual have been in historical Western Christianity as one of the most important rites in the church. Alan Richardson says:

> Theologically baptism signifies what God has done for our salvation through Christ and also what God does for men individually and corporately through the mediating work of Christ... The going down into the water symbolizes a burial and the coming up from the water a resurrection.[7]

---

[7] Alan Richardson (Ed.), *A Dictionary of Christian Theology* (Philadelphia: Westminster Press, 1969), p. 170.

It seems that the doctrine of the Trinity originated with the Council of Nicea in 325 A.D. Men such as Tertullian and Justin contributed to the development of the Trinity. One writer even credited Tertullian with the phrase, "One substance, three persons." That phrase has certainly helped to confuse comprehension of what the Trinity really is.

By way of definition, John Macquarrie says:

The Catholic faith is this. That we worship one God in trinity and trinity in unity; neither confounding the persons nor dividing the substance. For there is one person of the Father, another of the Son, and another of the Holy Ghost; but the Godhead of the Father, of the Son, and of the Holy Ghost is all one.

Macquarrie continues:

The unity of God is expressed in his one 'substance' or 'essence.' No person of the Trinity is any less God than the others; in particular, the Son and the Holy Spirit are not demigods or intermediaries, subordinate to the Father. [8]

The doctrine of the Trinity is not formally listed or contained in the Bible. The Trinity itself is more an attempt to glean inferences from the scriptures. One attempts to understand God as Father, Son and Holy Spirit. This doctrine has withstood the opposition of scattered minorities and continues to be a cardinal belief among many Western Christian followers. It is through

[8] John Macquarrie, *Principles of Christian Theology* (New York:Charles Scribner's Sons, 1966), pp. 174-186.

the doctrine of Trinity that one comes to understand the baptism formula "in the name of the Father, and of the Son, and of the Holy Spirit." There is, though, one group among the opposition that has steadfastly and sometimes vehemently denied the trinitarian doctrine and the trinitarian baptism. This group is the Black Apostolic church.

Contemporary Beliefs

The diversity of the Black Apostolic church has been reflected in its different organizations, and also in its divergent doctrinal beliefs. One can find doctrinal differences in practically all of the various organizations. Despite these minor differences there are points of emphasis that consistently designate all of them as Apostolics. These uniform tenets, it is believed, are adequately expressed in a statement printed in every issue of the *Shiloh Gospel Wave*. (This publication is the official organ of the Shiloh Apostolic Temple, Inc., headquartered in Philadelphia. Bishop Robert O. Doub, Jr., is the General Overseer.)

On the inside front page of every issue one can read the following:

Four Steps to Salvation: For all Nations to Obey to See God in Peace

1. Repent and be converted: Become godly sorry for our sins. Acts 3:19
2. Water Baptism: Be baptized in the name of Jesus Christ for the remission of sins. Acts 2:38
3. Holy Ghost: Everyone must receive the Holy Ghost with the Bible evidence of speaking in

another tongue according to the Holy Bible. Acts 2:4

4. Live a Holy Life: According to God's word. Hebrews 12:14.[9]

These are the basic doctrines for all going under the Apostolic banner today, with minor changes in wording by some groups.

As one considers some of the doctrines of the Apostolic church, it will be helpful to keep in mind that the primary effort here will concentrate on doctrinal points of similarity rather than the differences. While the differing tenets might be considered just as important as common tenets, it is the common points that define Apostolics as a group. It will help to look at these four steps as they are doctrinally emphasized in the Black Apostolic church.

1. *Repent and be converted.* If one were to label the theology of the Black Apostolic church, the terms "fundamental" and "conservative" comes to mind. There is belief in the depravity of man. Thousands of years of sin began with conduct of Adam and Eve and continue to be manifested today.

In the words of one Apostolic writer it is stated this way:

We believe that 'all men are sinners' not because they have committed any 'act' or 'acts' of sin, but by virtue of sin committed by the federal head of the human

---

[9] Robert O. Doub, ed., *Shiloh Gospel Wave.* (Philadelphia: Shiloh Apostolic Temple, August, 1972).

race, Adam... In Adam, 'all men sinned' ... his deprived rebellious nature became theirs in that they were yet in his loins... It is from this inbred, sinful nature that all acts of sin proceed. All men are in bondage, enslaved by sin. And no man has the power to deliver himself. This helpless, hopeless state caused the Apostle to cry, 'o wretched man that I am! Who shall deliver me from the body of this death? (Rom 7:25) His answer? Jesus Christ.[10]

Since all are born in sin because of Adam, then at some point in every believer's life repentance must take place. The person must acknowledge his sinful condition and ask forgiveness. There must also be an intention to change one's life. In the Discipline of the Church of Our Lord Jesus Christ, one notes these words:

> The only grounds upon which God will accept a sinner is Repentance from the heart for the sin that he has committed. A broken and contrite heart, He will not despise. (Ps 51:17). John preached Repentance. Jesus proclaimed it, and before His ascension commanded that 'Repentance and Remission of Sins should be preached in His name, beginning at Jerusalem.' (Lk 24:47). Peter fulfilled this command on the day of Pentecost. See Acts 2:38.[11]

Repentance or conversion is a very important concept in the doctrine of the Black Apostolic church.

---

[10] Morris E. Golder, *The Principles of Our Doctrine* (Indianapolis, Ind.: Grace Apostolic Church), p. 7.

[11] Robert C. Lawson, *Discipline Book, Church of Our Lord Jesus Christ.* (New York: Church of Christ Pub. Co., 19(9), p. 35.

The importance and meaning of this concept are essentially different in the Apostolic church than it is in the vast majority of churches affiliated with fundamental Protestantism. Others equate conversion to being saved. For Black Apostolics, however, repentance or conversion is turning from a sinful lifestyle toward God. One has now made the first step to obtain salvation.

What then are the other features that designate Black Apostolics? The answer points to the very heart, the very core of the Apostolic doctrine. The fact of sin has been established, the fact that men are born in sin. In spite of this, Apostolics teach that all can experience a new birth that is free of sin.

Apostolics generally hold to a literal interpretation of the scripture. As such, they believe Apostolic doctrine can, and in fact should, be substantiated by the Bible. In order to validate the authenticity of "being born again," one of the supportive scriptures is John 3:1-6. In these verses there is a record of a conversation between Jesus and a man named Nicodemus:

Now there was a man of the Pharisees, named Nicodemus, a ruler of the Jews. This man came to Jesus by night and said to him, 'Rabbi, we know that you are a teacher come from God; for no one can do these signs that you do, unless God is with him.' Jesus answered him, 'Truly, truly, I say to you, unless one is born anew, he cannot see the Kingdom of God.' Nicodemus said to him 'How can a man be born when he is old? Can he enter a second time into his mother's womb and be born?' Jesus answered, 'Truly, truly, I say to you, unless one is born of the *water* and the *spirit*, he *cannot* enter the kingdom of God. That which is born of the flesh is flesh and that which is born of the spirit is spirit.'[12]

Interpreted from the Apostolic viewpoint, being "born anew" or again is a universal statement by Jesus. Although he spoke to Nicodemus, the statement holds true for all people, everywhere, in all ages. Looking at the conversation through the Apostolic interpretation, one learns that' 'being born of the water and the spirit" is also very important. Water refers to baptism in the name of Jesus Christ, and Spirit refers to the baptism of the Holy Ghost, with the initial evidence of speaking in tongues. Apostolics attach monumental significance to this scripture because, "Unless one is born of water and the spirit, he cannot enter the kingdom of God." Whatever else the kingdom of God might mean to people, to Apostolics it means that at the judgment if one has not been born again, hell will be that person's eternal home.

Briefly some attention should be given to important steps to salvation in the Apostolic doctrine. When one indicates a desire to join an Apostolic church, he usually experiences water baptism before spirit baptism. There is nothing, however, that says it must happen that way. It is just that in the normal process of joining the church, the pastor and members assume the primary responsibility of baptizing the new candidates. Since the doctrine might be foreign to the person, subsequent additional teaching will usually precede the baptism of the spirit. If the candidate has grown up in the Apostolic church, water baptism may occur as young as five or six years old. Spirit baptism does not generally occur that early for believers.

---

[12] John 3:1-6. (RSV)

Because water baptism usually happens initially (as was mentioned in the four steps), many would choose to discuss this doctrinal point first. In the historical development of the Black Apostolic church, however, water baptism in Jesus' name is a later practice which developed subsequent to the 1906 Pentecostal experience. This writer will then focus on spirit baptism before discussing water baptism.

2. *Holy Spirit Baptism.* Many Apostolics compare physical birth to the spiritual birth to explain their doctrinal position. Just as it takes *two,* a male sperm and a female egg together, to bring about a new physical birth, so it takes two, water and spirit, in the spiritual birth. It is accepted that if a believer has not experienced both water and spirit baptism, that person has not in fact been born again.

Apostolics, as indeed all Pentecostals, validate and prove the reality of spirit baptism according to the occurrences described in the second chapter of Acts, the Day of Pentecost. However, another passage of scripture in the Apostolic interpretation preceded the Acts account. That scripture, attributed to Jesus, confirms the second chapter of Acts. The scriptural passage referred to is John 14:13-26. In this scripture, Apostolics contend that Jesus says he will be leaving the world shortly. His physical presence will no longer be around to support, counselor comfort his disciples. But Jesus will not leave his disciples spiritually defenseless. Therefore, the Holy Ghost, or the Holy Spirit will be sent:

... And I will pray the Father, and he will give you another Counselor, to be with you forever, even the Spirit of truth, whom the world cannot receive, because it neither sees him nor knows him; you know him for he dwells with you and will be in you.

I will not leave you desolate; I will come to you. Yet a little while and the world will see me no more, but you will see me; because I live, you will live also.

In that day you will know that I am in my Father, and you in me, and I in you.

... These things I have spoken to you, while I am still with you. But the Counselor, the Holy Spirit, whom the Father will send in my name, he will teach you all things, and bring to your remembrance all that I have said to you.... [13]

The Apostolic interpretation of doctrine is firmly absolutistic. Born and reared in this tradition, it becomes clear that the absolutistic point of view has been based on the King James Version of the scriptures. Certain words are emphasized only as they appear in the King James Version. References in the Apostolic interpretation and understanding must from time-to-time be made to the KJV.

The point is this. In the Revised Standard Version (RSV), the word *counselor* appears where the KJV offers the word *comforter*. And while as the two versions seem to suggest that the words can be used interchangeably or

---

[13] Ibid., John 14:16-20, 25-26

synonymously, the two would not necessarily be understood in the same light. The KJV is the dominant version used in all Apostolic congregations. Because most Apostolic laity have not used any other version of the scriptures, the Holy Ghost would be understood as more of a *Comforter* (providing encouragement, strength, even leadership) rather than a *counselor* (providing advice or supervision).

With these interpretive statements then, it is helpful to consider a part of the same scriptural passage from the KJV.

. .. And I will pray the Father, and he shall give you another Comforter, that he may abide with you forever...

I will not leave you comfortless: I will come to you...

These things have I spoken unto you, being yet present with you. But the Comforter, which is the Holy Ghost, whom the Father will send in my name, he shall teach you all things, and bring all things to your remembrance, whatsoever I have said unto you.[14]

As far as the Apostolic doctrine goes, it would not be inaccurate to say that the St. John 14:26 passage is considered as the prophetic words of Jesus. And his prophecy relates to the Day of Pentecost experience in Acts the second chapter.

The book of Acts teaches that the Holy Ghost empowers the believer. With this power, one is able to live

---

[14] John 14:16-18, 25-26. (KJV)

a morally-correct life, a spiritually-high life, and also witness to others with conviction and sincerity. The suggestion of power is found in Acts the first chapter:

> ... To them he presented himself alive after his passion by many proofs, appearing to them during forty days, and speaking of the Kingdom of God. And while staying with them he charged them not to depart from Jerusalem, but to wait for the promise of the Father, which, he said, you heard from me, for John baptized with water, but before many days you shall be baptized with the Holy Spirit... But you shall receive power when the Holy Spirit has come upon you; and you shall be my witness in Jerusalem and in all Judea and Samaria and to the end of the earth.[15]

After the Apostles had been instructed to tarry in Jerusalem, the Acts account indicates that Jesus was carried up to heaven on a cloud. Apostolics most definitely support the belief that in the "second coming" or the "second appearing," this same Jesus will descend to receive the church.

This waiting period that took place for the Apostles culminated with the glorious, spectacular, and unprecedented events that are recorded in the first few verses of Acts 2. This historical event has repeatedly been used by Pentecostals, neo-Pentecostals, and Apostolics alike, to justify the contemporary meaning and understanding of charismatic experience.

---

[15] Acts 1:3-5. (RSV)

In Acts 2 certain words are considered as important as the actual event. Prior to the historical believers' experiencing the actual speaking in tongues, there is mention of "tongues as a fire," as well as a "mighty wind." The KJV includes the word "cloven tongues as a fire." The word cloven has additional meaning for many Apostolics. This is noted in the RSV and KJV particular passages. Beginning with Acts 2:1, it reads:

> When the day of Pentecost had come, they were all together in one place. And suddenly a sound came from heaven like the rush of a mighty wind, and it filled all the house where they were sitting.
>
> And there appeared to them tongues as of fire, distributed and resting on each one of them.[16]

Turning now to the King James Version the same scriptural passage in Acts 2 reads like this:

> And when the day of Pentecost was fully come, they were all with one accord in one place. And suddenly there came a sound from heaven as of a rushing mighty wind, and it filled all the house where they were sitting. And there appeared unto them cloven tongues like as of fire, and it sat upon each of them.[17]

The reader will note that there was first the "rush" or "rushing mighty wind." Secondly, there appeared unto them "tongues" or "cloven tongues as of fire." The amazing thing is that the Acts report in several versions, indicates that some flame-looking substance touched each person.

---

[16] Ibid., Acts 2:1-3
[17] Acts 2:1-3 (KJV)

Practically all Pentecostals accept glossolalia as a normative experience. But Hoekema takes a somewhat different view. (Hoekema is not a Pentecostal.) He has difficulty accepting glossolalia as a normative experience. Hoekema's question is why should just speaking in tongues be considered the physical evidence? Why not the rushing mighty wind or the tongues as of fire?

Carl Brumback, a white Pentecostal with the Assemblies of God, gives a response in his work, *What Meaneth This?* According to Brumback.

> The sound 'as of a rushing mighty wind' and 'the cloven tongues like as of fire' were accompaniments of the Holy Spirit in His official descent from Heaven and in His outward and visible revelation of His presence ... The wind and fire were ... in the realm of nature ... and were never repeated after this occasion; on the other hand, speaking with tongues is the recorded accompaniment of several subsequent fillings with the Spirit in the books of Acts.[18]

Brumback feels that the wind and fire were important in the New Testament church's initial experience of the Spirit baptism. His contention is that these dramatic accompaniments have not been needed since.

Apostolics have incorporated opposite views in this doctrinal development of the cloven tongues. There is little or nothing said about any interpretative belief about the winds. But cloven tongues are considered very

---

[18] Carl Brumback, op. cit., pp. 198-199.

significant. Prior to having the actual tongue-speaking experience, it is taught that many seekers or believers experience a sort of incoherent "gibberish." During this period, one may in fact be under the anointing of the spirit, but not become possessed by the spirit. This anointed "gibberish" is said to' be cloven tongues.

The group that supports this concept feels that a person is almost ready to "speak" but has not quite sacrificed all for the Holy Ghost to come in. When total surrender to the spirit takes place, the spirit comes in with the physical evidence of speaking in tongues. Some Apostolics thus believe that cloven tongues are being manifested today just as speaking in tongues is being manifested.

On the other hand, there are other Apostolics who believe that cloven tongues as of fire were only evidenced on the Day of Pentecost. This group maintains that this particular phenomenon has only taken place once and has never been repeated. According to this group of Apostolics, not only has cloven tongues not been repeated, but the rushing wind also has never been repeated. So then, some Apostolics share a belief with Brumback and some do not.

No such diversity exists among Apostolics when they move to the fourth verse of Acts. For the most part, there is total unanimity of belief. Focusing on Acts 2:4, one finds these words:

> And they were all filled with the Holy Spirit and began to speak in other tongues, as the Spirit gave them utterance (RSV).

This verse is "part and parcel," "bread and butter," of the Apostolic doctrine. This verse supports, substantiates and validates the doctrinal belief of spirit baptism with tongue speaking. Apostolic churches observe testimony meetings, and one of the favorite statements in most testimonies goes something like this:

I thank the Lord for the baptism of (or the gift of) the Holy Ghost, according to Acts 2:4.

Making this statement reassures the other brothers and sisters that one has been "saved" and is still going on with the Lord.

In his booklet, *The Principles of Our Doctrine,* Morris E. Golder speaks on this subject. Bishop Golder, is the official church historian of the Pentecostal Assemblies of the World and was the first Apostolic seminary-trained minister whom this writer was privileged to hear. Talking about the doctrine, he has this to say:

We believe that speaking with tongues as the spirit gives utterance is the initial evidence of the indwelling of the spirit; not only on the day of Pentecost, for the one hundred and twenty, but for all believers for all time... Speaking with tongues is the 'sound' of the spirit heard by EVERY believer. It is synonymous with the cry of the 'newborn babe' in the first birth (flesh); for God has sent forth His birth into our hearts in the Second Birth (of Spirit). 19[19]

---

[19] Morris Golder, op. cit., p. 12.

This position by Golder is supported by nearly all Apostolics. The disciplines of most Apostolic organizations reflect the agreement of Apostolics on this issue. In the *Bible Way Church Rules Book,* the following statements on baptism of the Spirit are noted:

> **The Baptism of ihe Holy Ghost is the Birth of the Spirit** (John 3:5); that spiritual baptism is necessary to put anyone into the kingdom of God (God's true church; the Bride of Christ), and is evidenced by speaking in Other Tongues (other languages) as the Spirit of God gives utterance. [20]

Contrary to the belief of some, the passage in Acts 2:4 is not the only verse used to support a belief in glossolalia. Other passages in the book of Acts are also significant. One must also understand that most Apostolics are dispensationalists. This belief holds that people are now living in the Grace Dispensation. In this regard, the Day of Pentecost "happening" is believed to have been the initial work of the Holy Spirit in this dispensation. Dispensationalism teaches that since the Jews were God's "chosen people" in the Old Testament, this experience came to them first in Jerusalem on the Day of Pentecost.

Apostolics feel that if the experience had been limited to the Jews in Jerusalem, there would not be sufficient reason to hold that tongues was meant to be universal. Apostolics claim that this experience is for all peoples everywhere.

---

[20] Smallwood Williams (Ed.), Rules and Regulations of the Bible Way Church of Our Lord Jesus Christ World Wide. Washington, D.C.: Bible Way Church Press, 1962.

Continuing in the second chapter of Acts, at the fifth verse, one notes these words:

> Now there were dwelling in Jerusalem Jews, devout men from every nation under heaven. And at this Sound (speaking in tongues) the multitude came together, and they were bewildered, because each one heard them speaking in his own language. And they were amazed and marveled...[21]

Paying specific attention to the sixth verse, Apostolic doctrine notes that all those who were able to understand the Galileans included Parthians, Medes, Elamites, residents of Mesopotamia, Judea, Cappadocia, Pontus, Asia, Egypt, Rome and Arabia (Acts 2:9-14). The known world was pretty well represented, and all understood. These are the universal implications.

The Galileans did in fact speak in tongues. While there has not been such comprehension by hearers since, the first occasion verified two things. First it proved that these Galileans were definitely God-sent. Secondly, because all the hearers understood this God-inspired act, this proved that the experience was available to all, Jews and Gentile alike.

There is more scriptural support. In the tenth chapter of Acts, one reads that Peter visited the house of Cornelius in Caesarea. This supports the belief that tongue-speaking is universal. Unlike the Acts 2:4 account,

---

[21] Acts 2:5-7 (RSV)

the people in Caesarea were Gentiles not Jews. Acts 10:42-46 highlights the points.

> ... And he commanded us to preach to the people, and to testify that he is the one ordained by God to be judge. To him all the prophets bear witness that everyone who believes in him receives forgiveness of sins through his name. While Peter was still saying this the Holy Spirit fell on all who heard the word. And the believers from among the circumcised (the Jews) who came with Peter were amazed, because the gift of the Holy Spirit had been poured out even on the Gentiles. For they heard them speaking in tongues and extolling God. [22]

This event proves for Apostolics that the experience of receiving the Holy Ghost was essentially the same for Jews and Gentiles. The accompanying sign in both cases was speaking in tongues.

A third passage in Acts 19: 1-7 shows that all who receive the Holy Ghost *must* speak in tongues and that God intended all to have the experience:

> While Apollos was at Corinth, **Paul** passed through the upper country and came to Ephesus. And he said to them, Did you receive the Holy Spirit when you believed? ... And when Paul had laid his hands upon them, the Holy Spirit came on them; and they spoke with tongues and prophesied. There were about twelve of them in all.[23]

---

[22] Ibid., Acts 10:42-46.
[23] Ibid., Acts 19:1-2, 6-7.

In his book, *Understanding Speaking in Tongues,* Watson Mills says this about tongues at Caesarea and Ephesus:

> ... Probably because the case involving Cornelius is unique, Luke dwells upon it at length... He is careful to indicate clearly that this gentile convert (Cornelius) received the Spirit in exactly the same manner as did the Jewish disciples at Pentecost...

> Similarly, the incident of glossolalia at Ephesus was Luke's way of indicating that God's approval rested upon the experience of the people there.[24]

Apostolics believe scriptural support exists for receiving the Holy Ghost and speaking in tongues as a normative experience for all Christians.

Since speaking in tongues is the initial physical evidence of the baptism of the Holy Ghost, how does one deal with Paul's writings on tongues in I Corinthians, Chapters 12-14. Apostolics have also dealt with that question. What has resulted is a belief that tongues in Acts and tongues in Corinthians are different. Tongues in Acts are thought to be the *evidence of the spirit;* in I Corinthians, tongues are thought to be a *gift of the spirit.*

Morris Golder provides some insight:

> We hold that there is a vast difference between (1) 'speaking in *Other* tongues as the Spirit gives utterance,' (2) the Gift of Tongues as mentioned by St.

---

[24] Watson Mills, *Understanding Speaking in Tongues* (Grand Rapids, Mich.: Wm. B. Eerdmans Pub. Co., 1972), pp. 38-39.

Paul's letter to the Corinthians (12-14). Speaking in other tongues as the spirit gives utterance is supernatural, Spirit-enforced sign or witness of the Spirit's indwelling ...

The Gift of Tongues called also 'unknown tongues' mentioned by St. Paul is an endowment given by the Holy Ghost along with other 'spiritual gifts.' (I Cor. 12:7-11). It is one of the gifts given by the Spirit for the edification of the believer himself (I Cor. 14:4) and for the edification of the church where there is an interpreter present (I Cor. 14:27-28) ...

Golder then offers these words of summary that more accurately state the doctrinal position:

Speaking in tongues as the Spirit gives utterance is the experience common to ALL believers, while the gift of tongues is given by the Spirit to those He wills to endow.[25]

Water Baptism

"Unless you get baptized in Jesus' name, you don't have it the right way, according to the scriptures." This statement can be heard countless times in any Black Apostolic church. It is recited by ministers and laity alike with conviction, confidence, and enthusiasm. On various other doctrinal points, Apostolics can be lumped or labeled with other Protestants or other Pentecostals. But the Apostolic belief about baptism is a distinguishing doctrine. It is considered to be a primary Apostolic feature.

---

[25] Morris Golder, pp. 2-13.

Strangely enough, Apostolics often use Matthew 28:19 as a point of departure because they feel an error has been made in the interpretation of the Matthew 28:19 passage. Apostolics do not interpret this as a textual formula for baptism. It is rather understood as a general command to do something.

Apostolics believe the command was fully obeyed for the first time during the events recorded in the latter part of the second chapter of Acts. Apostolics contend that Jesus' command to baptize "all nations in the name of the Father and of the Son, and of the Holy Spirit" was carried out when they were baptized "in the name of Jesus" in Acts 2:38. While the Matthew text is not regarded as formulaic, the Acts 2:38 text is regarded as historical use of a formula:

> Let all the house of Israel therefore know assuredly that God has made him both Lord and Christ. This Jesus whom you crucified. Now when they heard this, they were cut to the heart, and said to Peter and the rest of the Apostles, Brethren, what shall we do?
>
> And Peter said to them, Repent, and be baptized every one of you in the name of Jesus Christ for the forgiveness of your sins; and you shall receive the gift of the Holy Spirit ... So those who received his word were baptized, and there were added that day about three thousand souls.[26]

This text is primary for Apostolics, who believe the "name of the Father, Son, and Holy Spirit" is Jesus. Other

---

[26] Acts 2:36-38, 41. (RSV)

scriptures also confirm belief in Jesus' name baptism. In the *Book of Church Order and Discipline of the United Church of Jesus Christ (Apostolic),* Bishop Monroe Saunders says this about baptism:

> We baptize in the name of Jesus Christ because it is Apostolic in origin and practice (Acts 2:38; 8:12-17; 10:47, 48; 19:1-6).
> ... No other mode of baptism is to be found in the New Testament. For more than one hundred years after Pentecost, believers were baptized only in the Name, Jesus Christ.

Lest there be some doubt concerning the command that Jesus gave his apostles, Saunders adds this:

> ... In Matthew 28:19, we have a commission, or a command *given;* in Acts 2:38, we have the command *executed.* In the former, the apostles were told *what* to do, in the latter, they *did* it.[27]

In addition to the scripture in the second chapter of Acts, Saunders lists three others in the book of Acts. The second scripture is Acts 8:12-17. In this passage, Phillip, who had gone to Samaria to preach, was subsequently joined by Peter and John.

> But when they believed Phillip as he preached good news about the Kingdom of God and the name of Jesus Christ they were baptized, both men and women... Now when the apostles at Jerusalem heard that Samaria had received the word of God, they sent to

---

[27] Monroe R. Saunders, *Church Order and Discipline of the United Church of Jesus Christ (Apostolic)* (Washington, D.C., 1965), pp. 21-22.

them Peter and John, who came down and prayed for them that they might receive the Holy Spirit; for it had not yet fallen on any of them, but they had only been baptized in the name of the Lord Jesus. Then they laid hands on them and they received the Holy Spirit.[28]

This scripture is important for Apostolics because it demonstrates that the Samaritans (a mixed group of people considered as societal outcasts) were included as God's people along with Jews and Gentiles. And further evidence of Gentile inclusion is shown in the following passage:

While Peter was still saying this, the Holy Spirit fell on all who heard the word... Then Peter declared, can anyone forbid water for baptizing these people who have received the Holy Spirit?... And he commanded them to be baptized in the name of Jesus Christ. [29]

Whereas some think Paul raises points of difference with Peter on tongue speaking, they are in agreement on water baptism.

While Apollos was at Corinth, Paul passed through the upper country and came to Ephesus. There he found some disciples. And he said to them, Did you receive the Holy Spirit when you believed? And they said, No, we have never ever heard that there is a Holy Spirit. And he said Unto what then were you baptized? They said, Unto John's baptism. And Paul said John baptized with the baptism of repentance, telling the people to believe in the one who was to come after

---

[28] Acts 8:12, 14-17. (RSV).
[29] Ibid., Acts 10:44,47-48.

him, that is Jesus. On hearing this, they were baptized in the name of the Lord Jesus. And when Paul had laid his hands upon them, the Holy Spirit came on them...[30]

These scriptures prove for Apostolics that baptism should and must be administered in the name of Jesus.

It is certainly clear that if water baptism is to be administered at all in the Christian church, the correct formula should be "in the name of Jesus Christ."

Apostolics view the words, Father, Son and Holy Spirit as titles denoting God's different relationships to his creation and his creatures. But all Apostolics agree that when the Apostles followed Jesus' command (Matt 28:19), they did baptize in the name of all three titles. Apostolics understand the correct name to be Jesus. We note the following:

Father is not a proper name, nor son, nor Holy Ghost. Father expresses a relationship, also Son; and the Holy Ghost means the Holy Spirit, but does not mean His name but His nature. 'Holy' is an adjective meaning 'more excellence,' 'pure in heart,' and Spirit is a noun but not a proper name. So, they that baptize in the (trinitarian) formula ... do not baptize in any name at all.

... Jesus said, Go ye therefore and teach all nations, baptizing them in the name - not names, but name (one) of the Father and of the Son and of the Holy Ghost, and if there is none other Name under heaven

---

[30] Ibid. Acts 19:1-6.

164

given among men whereby we must be saved but Jesus Christ (Acts 4:12), then if we have not been baptized in the name of Jesus Christ, then we have not been baptized in the name of the Father, Son and Holy Ghost.[31]

In addition to the above words by the late Bishop R. C. Lawson, using in part Acts 4:12, Apostolics give other scriptures for Jesus' name baptism. Apostolics believe that salvation is only in Jesus Christ, and that Jesus is also the Lord.

Therefore, God has highly exalted him and bestowed on him the name which is above every name, that at the name of Jesus every knee should bow, in heaven and on earth and under the earth and every tongue confess that Jesus Christ is Lord, to the glory of God the Father.[32]

According to Apostolic interpretation, the scripture in the second chapter of Philippians emphasizes the importance of the name of Jesus. Therefore, baptism must be in the name of Jesus Christ. In addition to Paul's emphasis on Jesus in his epistle to Philippi, he also stresses the name of Jesus again in his epistle to the assembly of Colossae.

... Let the word of Christ dwell in you richly, as you teach and admonish one another in all wisdom, and as you sing psalms and hymns and spiritual songs with thankfulness in your hearts to God. And whatever you do in word or deed, do everything in the name of the

---

[31] Robert C. Lawson, *op. cit.,* pp. 29-30.
[32] Philippians 2:9-11. (RSV).

Lord Jesus, giving thanks to God the Father through him.[33]

Apostolics take this literally to mean that almost everything must be done in Jesus' name. There is no question about the fact that baptism is certainly one of the things to be done in the name.

If one used the New Testament as a basis for belief, then baptism in Jesus' name is more accurate than the more traditional trinitarian formula.

Jehovah of the Old Testament is Jesus of the New Testament

Interwoven with the Apostolic belief of Jesus' name baptism is an even more controversial doctrine. Even as Unitarian-Universalists deny the doctrine of the Trinity, so do Apostolics. But the reasons are different. Whereas Unitarians do not accept the Trinity because they do not believe Jesus was divine, or God, Apostolics refute the Trinity because they believe Jesus is God. In other words, in the Black Apostolic church a major doctrine is that Jehovah - God of the Old Testament is Jesus Christ of the New Testament.

According to Morris Golder, the Trinity is a part of historical Christianity, the post-biblical ages.

We repudiate and deny that the doctrine of the Trinity is substantiated by the word of God. It is true that it is a part of the great heritage of what is known as 'historical Christianity;' however, Apostolic

---

Pentecostals do not accept all that Christendom has embraced historically... the 'doctrine of the trinity' must be read into the sacred text. The Bible is the book of 'One God' who has revealed Himself in many ways.[34]

The One-God idea has always permeated the whole of Black Apostolic church doctrine. There has always been just one God. He has, however, taken on or been known by different names at different times.

While God was known by other names in previous dispensations (i.e., Jehovah, Yahweh), in the dispensation of Grace his name is Jesus. And because God's correct name is Jesus, Apostolics call on him by that name. While non-Apostolics have accused this group of putting too much emphasis on the second person of the Trinity, Apostolics have not meant it that way at all. For Jesus is not the second person of a divine Trinity; Jesus is all.

To merely state this thesis as doctrine without biblical proof would, for Apostolics, make it false. Diligent efforts have been put forth over the years to point out parallel scripture from the Old Testament and from the New Testament which prove that Jesus is God. Bishop R. C. Lawson did one of the most thorough jobs in this regard. He compared over one hundred passages of scripture in the Old and New Testaments.

It is not necessary to duplicate the entire list, but a sample list of some of the scriptures will illustrate.

---

[34] Morris Golder, *op. cit.,* pp. 5-6.

Jehovah God of the Old Testament is Jesus Christ of the New Testament

This is proven by the Creation
- Genesis 1:1; Isaiah 44:23, 24, compared with John 1:1, 10.
- 127 Genesis. 1:1. In the Beginning God created the heavens and the earth.
- John 1:1,10. In the beginning was the word and the word was God.

vs. 10 - He was in the world, and the world was made through him, yet the world knew him not.

This is proven by His Incarnation
- Isaiah 7:14, 9:6, compared with Matthew 1:18-25.

- Genesis 3:15, Psalm 68:21; Luke 8:11; John 1:2-14; Matthew 1:22-25; Galatians 3:16.

- Isaiah 7:14. Therefore the Lord himself will give you a sign. Behold, a young woman shall conceive and bear a son and shall call his name Immanuel.

- Matthew 1:18-25. Now the birth of Jesus Christ took place in this way. When his mother Mary had been betrothed to Joseph, before they came together, she was found to be with child of the Holy Spirit; and her husband Joseph, being a just man and unwilling to put her to shame, resolved to divorce her quietly. But as he considered this, behold, an angel of the Lord appeared to him in a dream, saying, 'Joseph, son of David, do not fear to take Mary your wife... Behold, a virgin shall conceive and bear a son, and his name shall be called Emmanuel' (which means, God with us).

The two areas mentioned in detail give an idea of how Lawson constructed his parallel scriptures. For the rest of his chart, a shorter version will be given.

This is proven by the works that He did
- Matthew 11:2-7, compared with Isaiah. 35:3-10; John 9:1-4; 14:11.

This is proven by His crucifixion
- Zachariah. 12:1, 10, compared with St. John 19:31-38; Acts 20:28.

This is proven by His burial
- Psalms. 74:12, compared with Matthew 12:40; Ephesians 4:7-10; I Peter 3:18-21; I Peter 4:4, 5.

This is proven by His resurrection
- Psalms 68:1, 16-19; Ephesians 4:7-12; Colossians. 2:9-11.

This is proved by His ascension
- Psalms 47:5-9, compared with Acts 1:9-11; I Thessalonians 4:13-17.

This is proven by His second coming
- Psalms 50: 1-8, compared with I Thessalonians 4: 13-17; Titus 2:11-14; I John 3:1-5; Zach. 14:3-6;

Habakkuk 3:3-6; Revelation 1:7-8; 19:11-18; compared with I Timothy 6:14-16.

This is proven by prophecy fulfilled
- II Peter 1:19-21; Isaiah 40:3-4, compared with Matthew 3:1-4, John 1:19-27.

The preceding list of scriptures showing that Jesus is God is taken from the Discipline Book, The Church of Our Lord Christ. Bishop R. C. Lawson, who founded the organization, wrote this book of doctrine and discipline.)

In addition to Lawson's, men such as the late Bishop S.C. Johnson, Bishop Tilman Carmichael and C. P. Kilgore compiled scriptures on this subject. Bishop Johnson's pamphlet has since been edited and revised by Bishop S. McDowell Shelton.

This particular doctrine presents no major problem in dealing with the incarnation. Apostolics feel that since God found no one worthy to reclaim the world, he chose to do it himself. By impregnating Mary, God was able to assume some human form. He thus became Jesus in the flesh. This was done, however, without abandoning or sacrificing any of his divine nature or divine powers. While Apostolics will acknowledge that Jesus the Man was not omnipresent, there is no question but that he was omnipotent and omniscient.

It is believed that the physical body that Jesus used was a temporary "temple" while he lived on earth. The death, destruction, or termination of the physical body did not in any way limit Jesus because he still had the infinite spirit. And while the spirit dwelled in the body, it also existed outside of the body. Today it is that omnipotent spirit of Jesus, that is God.

You Must be Holy

In the Black Apostolic church all believers must repent, be baptized in Jesus' name, and speak in tongues as the initial evidence of the Holy Ghost. After all of this has happened, the believer has been "born again."

With this new birth, one begins to live a new and different life. One is ready to live holy and sanctified. The passage of scripture most frequently quoted as supportive of a holy life is Hebrews 12:14. The Revised Standard Version reads:

Strive for peace with all men, and for the holiness without which no one will see the Lord.

The KJV version of Hebrews 12:14 reads like this:

Follow peace with all men and holiness, without which no man shall see the Lord.

The emphasis on holiness and living the holy life has always been extremely important. This holiness that the biblical writers speak of is understood to be a life style free of "worldly" things. One cannot live holy unless one is sanctified. And while sanctification (a spiritual cleansing) necessarily precedes the Holy Ghost, the believer is better equipped to live holy after receiving the Holy Ghost. This is so because one receives power after the Holy Ghost has come (Acts 1:8). According to the Apostolic doctrine, not only does this power enable one to witness convincingly, but it also enables one to live the kind of life that is "sin free."

While Apostolics all believe in holiness, they do not agree on what is, in fact, included in a holy life. There are various organizational interpretations of ethical standards.

For Apostolics, the holy life really becomes a list of "do's and don'ts." Each organization lists numbers of things that the bishop or the board of bishops considers to be sinful or wrong. Matters of dress and recreation, women preachers, and divorce and remarriage illustrate pertinent disagreements among Black Apostolics.

The Pentecostal Assemblies of the World is considered one of the more conservative Apostolic organizations. However, labeling a group as conservative, moderate or liberal is unfair since it always depends on the issue debated.

How members dress has always been considered to be an accurate gauge of holiness. Most Apostolic organizations put emphasis on "proper" dress for men and women. Most of the points, however, are related to women. The women in PAW do not wear noticeable makeup or jewelry. Short skirts are also considered inappropriate. Men are encouraged to dress conservatively.

Also, in the Believer's Guide Book for the Apostle Church of Christ In God one notes some specifics in terms of what is considered wrong or unholy.

All members of the... Apostle Church of Christ In God should adorn themselves as becoming Saints (I Timothy 2:9-10)

... Now in order to dress as becoming Saints, one should wear a nice length dress, not a mini dress, which make us look like the world.

Under Rule 5 in the same category, more specifies can be found:

... Other accessories, namely beads, earrings, finger nail polish, lipstick, etc., are worn because of pride (I John 2:16; II Kings 30:33); and they should not be used

... There is to be no dancing in your homes or elsewhere for the devil. We only dance in the Spirit for the Lord. (II Samuel 6:14; Psalms 149:3).[35]

There is also an uncompromising position on abortion. The only exception to this hard and fast rule is when the mother's health is endangered.

The area of recreation in many instances, is labeled sin. The church leadership of PAW ultimately leaves the final decision on such matters to the pastor and the local assembly. This guideline is suggested though:

... The question for a Christian must not always be whether a course of action (recreation) be positively immoral, but whether it will dull the spiritual life and

---

[35] James C. Richardson, Sr., *Believers' Guide Book for the Mt. Sinai Apostle Church of Christ in God* (Martinsville, Va., 1973), pp. 2-3.

be an unwise example. Thus, causing the cause of Christ to be evilly spoken of. [36]

Translated for local congregations, many consider sinful such recreational activities as bowling, swimming, basketball and the like.

Women preachers have been an issue of contention also. Some Apostolics do not believe women should preach or "usurp authority" over men.

The Pentecostal Assemblies of the World, while strict about matters of dress, has been one of the more liberal Apostolic groups in encouraging women in ministry. PAW has had women serving as pastors of local congregations throughout the country. The church leaders of PAW have long been cognizant of the effective leadership role assumed by many women. Rather than restrict them, the women were encouraged to enter the pastorate.

The Church-of Our Lord Jesus Christ of the Apostolic Faith's founder, R. C. Lawson, originally split from PAW on matters of women ministers and divorce and remarriage. Lawson disagreed with the position of PAW. Thus, in the Church of Our Lord Jesus Christ, women have never been appointed to pastorships, nor have they ever been ordained.

Divorce and remarriage at times has been a very volatile issue in many other Apostolic organizations as

---

[36] 36 Paul A. Bowers, 1972 *Minute Book of the Pentecostal Assemblies of the World* (Indianapolis, Ind., 1972), pp. 52-53.

well. In a 1952 meeting of PAW these statements were made relative to divorce and remarriage:

> Section 9. To establish a standard, governing marriage and divorce; our standard to be that there shall be no divorce and remarriage where both have or have had the baptism of the Holy Ghost.[37]

The preceding statement is under the section headed "doctrine." And in the same book under the heading "Laws," one also notes the following:

> Section 14. We recommend that all P.A. of W. ministers discourage divorce, even though fornication is a proven fact, if the guilty party still wishes to remain with his companion and is willing to discontinue his improper conduct and that divorce be only a last resort. Adopted)[38]

That law passed at the 1952 convention. However, a check of the 1972 Minute Book shows there is still obviously some problem relative to divorce. Here we can observe:

> (c) The innocent party should not exercise his right to divorce form a sinning companion except as a last resort. (I Cor 7:28). Loosing is possible but should not be sought after. We have the example of godliness in this respect in God's dealing with Israel (Jer. 3:6, 8). He did not divorce her until all his overtures had been

[37] R. L. Robinson, *Minutes, Pentecostal Assemblies of the World* (Indianapolis, Ind., 1952), p. 27.
[38] Ibid., p. 32.

refused, even though her fornication was a proven and openly know fact.[39]

The PAW board of bishops is not categorically opposed to divorce. However, they stress the demonstration of as much understanding as possible.

In order to get a clear historical picture of the divorce issue, one must examine the Haywood and Lawson positions. As first presiding bishops of PA W and COOLJC respectively, these two did much to shape and mold the Black Apostolic doctrine. One must also remember that the PAW stance on divorce was paramount in Lawson's decision to withdraw from that church group.

To see what that stance was, one should note the booklet The Marriage and Divorce Question, by Bishop G. T. Haywood. Haywood says: "The contents of this booklet is to prove that persons who divorced and remarried before they were filled with the Holy Spirit are forgiven of their past, and a new life begins."[40] 40

Bishop Haywood commented, "In times past I have been very dogmatic upon the subject (of divorce) and have said many things which I afterward was made to stop and consider. I have studied the subject very carefully and prayerfully. Some things were a puzzle to me. It was strange that after we preached that a man, or woman, living with a formerly divorced companion, was living in adultery, yet God could baptize them with the Holy Ghost

---

[39] Paul A. Bowers, op. cit., p. 51.

[40] G. T. Haywood, The Marriage and Divorce Question in the Church, (Indianapolis, Ind.), p. 2.

in spite of all that we had said or done against them. I had preached many a time and caused many of them to separate ... But one day God halted me ... and I surrendered."[41]

Bishop Haywood felt that divorce had to be looked at in different perspectives. First, he said the biblical record does not apply to the world. Therefore, church leaders cannot expect those outside of the church to be governed by rules for the church. Secondly, Haywood believed that two born again individuals in the church had no grounds for divorce. As Haywood put it, "in the Church there is to be. no divorcing and remarrying among the Children of God."

As this writer understands Bishop Haywood's position, those who were divorced prior to experiencing new birth were not under grace but under law (of the land). The scriptures were not applicable to them.

PAW (Haywood's church group) uses fornication alone as a reason for divorce among church members.
Fornication used here however, has a meaning broader than just a sexual connotation.

In the 1976 Minute Book of the Pentecostal Assemblies of the World, we find the following:

The sixth verse of Matthew 19 is not an all-embracing prohibition of divorce. It simply means that the male and female were ordained of God to be one flesh. A

---

[41]Ibid., p. 5.

strange person whether man or woman, entering in confuses and disrupts the oneness which God intended should be. Therefore... the divorce decree is a mere legal recognition of the havoc already wrought.

Continuing, we observe, "so much depends upon the proper interpretation of the key term, 'fornication.' Present day dictionaries teach us that fornication is the sexual act indulged in by unmarried persons. But the force of the term, as used in the Scriptures, was not so restricted. The Greek verb forming the root of the disputed term is 'Porneu' meaning, the indulgence of all unlawful sex desires. Thus, we see fornication is a general term applying to many unlawful indulgences. The Scriptures confirm this assertion; I Cor. 5: 1... and Romans 1:26, 27, 29.

Section 9 ask all PAW ministers, to discourage divorce, and that it be used only as a last resort."[42]

PAW rules do not categorically prevent remarriage after divorce; that is as long as one spouse was not saved at the time of the separation.

Turning now to the R. C. Lawson school of thought we get a somewhat different picture. In the *Discipline* of the Church of Our Lord Jesus Christ of the Apostolic Faith 1955, we note that Bishop Lawson says, "Jesus did away with the divorce law and restored matrimony back to the Edenic standard. Matthew 19:3-8."

---

[42] Paul A. Bowers, 1976 *Minute Book of the Pentecostal Assemblies of the World* (Indianapolis, Ind., 1976), pp. 16-18.

Lawson added, "Under the New Testament no court on earth should dissolve the marriage relation. (Mk 10:2-9; Matt 19:5-6) ... husband and wife are bound together for life; death alone severs the marriage tie. (Rom 7:2-3; I Cor 7:39)."[43]

The Lawson position does allow for divorce, but even then, remarriage is forbidden. "There is but one cause for which a man can put away his wife. (But) After a man has lawfully put away his wife, or a wife has put away her husband, they are positively forbidden to marry again until the former companion is dead. (Mk 10:11-12, Lk 16:18, Rom. 7:23)."[44]

The Lawson position is adamant against divorce. It should not take place. If, however, it does occur then the innocent party cannot remarry.

This doctrinal interpretation is still practiced by the COOLJC.

Many more organizations could be listed. And each would have a list of abstentions. While persons may agree or disagree with the lists, the overall purpose is for one to show and to see a difference in one's own life. For, according to the doctrine of the Black Apostolic church, every believer must do four things: The believer must repent, must be baptized in water in the name of Jesus Christ, must receive the Holy Ghost with the initial evidence of speaking in tongues, and finally, every believer must live a holy, sanctified life.

---

[43] Robert C. Lawson, *Discipline Book of the Church of Our Lord Jesus Christ* (New York City, 1955), pp. 36-38.

[44] Ibid., pp. 38-39.

The late Bishop Robert C. Lawson summarized it this way:

> We believe that in order to escape the judgement of God and to have the hope of enjoying the glory of life eternal, one must be thoroughly saved from his (her) sins, sanctified unto God and filled with the Holy Ghost, and that a wholly sanctified life is the only true stand of a Christian Life (Heb. 12:14, I Pet. 1:15-17).[45]

.

---

[45] Ibid., p. 46.

CHAPTER 4

CONCLUSIONS

The underlying thrust of this book has been to present a survey of the history and teachings of the Black Apostolic denominations. While this is a rapidly growing movement, there is a scarcity of written information about it. Further, schisms happen frequently and are considered by the author to be a serious problem. It is inconceivable that organizations function better from incessant splits and needles duplication. For the church especially, this kind of negative action lessens the church's effectiveness in performing its mission. Respect is hard to gain when an organization or institution functions in such a fragmented, absurd way. What then can be done about the countless number of splits that occur in the Black Apostolic church? Let us consider the varied reasons that have been given for the splits.

Doctrinal differences are often used to justify splits. One group might say that wearing of makeup by women is not necessarily sinful. A very fundamental minister (who feels that he is a little holier than the rest) expresses a belief that such is not "becoming to holiness." What usually happens is that this minister and his group will issue an ultimatum to the organizational board, or the presiding bishop. "Either the women stop wearing makeup or we will leave." In most cases the dissenting group leaves.

Two things should be considered relative to doctrine. First, disagreement centers on differing interpretations of scripture or doctrine. Because one side claims a superior interpretation of the Bible, reconciliation is usually very difficult.

Secondly, when the dissident group leaves, a new organization is nearly always started, rather than the dissidents aligning themselves with an existing Apostolic organization. In many cases, differences that caused the split cease to be visible after the split. The schismatic group looks more like the former group than a different group.

Another reason for schism is administrative differences. Interpreted by many who have used this reason for leaving, it means there are not enough "bishops' hats" to go around. It seems everybody wants to wear the title of bishop. Dissidents rarely leave in protest of "poor" organization. Few seem to be concerned with making the organization more efficient. Administrative differences seldom seem to include concern for an organized approach to assisting new congregations in initial efforts. Dissidents seldom leave over major administrative concerns about the purpose and mission of the church in these contemporary times. Instead, even when a dissatisfied minister has no doctrinal disagreement, the desire to be elevated to the bishopric is sufficient reason, he thinks, to start his own organization. The existing organization may already have an ample supply of bishops. But there exists within the corporate mentality of Apostolic clergy a kind of hunger and thirst for the bishopric, a "lust for the power of office." Many covet the office without any thought as to personal qualifications or need. Organizations of only twenty-five or thirty churches might have as many as eight bishops to oversee its affairs.

While the need for more competent bishops is prevalent, there must surely be a more effective way to find these persons.

Why Splits are Destructive

Apostolics need to prayerfully consider the implications of all these divisions. Schisms often imply a lack of genuine love and understanding on the part of leaders. They also indicate a limited ability to compromise and tolerate divergent opinions and views. This "split syndrome" also implies a lack of vision.

The smaller the group, the more it tends to revolve around a central personality, the presiding bishop. Presiding bishops are often aware of this. Are these bishops more interested in perpetuating themselves than "God's program?"

Yet another problem results from the consistent dividing of the church. It weakens the effectiveness of the message that Apostolics present. The belief that the Apostolic church represents true Christianity is lost beneath a pile of competing personalities and organizations. When one is convinced that the Apostolic church is "the way," there is still a problem. One is confronted with literally "a maze of Apostolic ways." Which is the better way? The PAW, COOLJC, ACCG, BWWW, or some other Apostolic organization?

In the midst of this, Apostolics maintain an absolutistic point of view. "You either come our way or you are going to hell." The writer, however, considers this attitude an affront and an insult to God. It is difficult to understand how splintered, terribly divisive, and sometimes self-defeating Apostolic organizations can each claim to be the only instrumentality of God in such a day and time as this.

God's word must be declared regardless of the condition of one's own house. But it is still true that one's deeds are more respected than one's words. If Black Apostolic organizations would begin major efforts toward ecumenicity, their message would be more effective. Above all, the Apostolic church's claim to be the representative of God will be more genuine.

How Can the "Split Syndrome" be Alleviated?

The author is aware that some organizations are so enamored in their own success that uniting is thought to be fruitless. The following options should be considered by those who are concerned about the lack of Apostolic unity.

An initial meeting of the organizational heads is necessary. The plan, program, and participation in this meeting should include as many different organizations as possible. The meeting could take the form of a congress, a national fellowship meeting, seminars or workshops. The meeting should explore points of unity, with secondary attention to points of disunity.

Contact with the different Apostolic organizations in follow-up would be extremely vital. This writer thus sees the need for the creation of a National Apostolic Liaison Office. The duties of the office would be manifold:

1. To set up all future meetings on an interorganizational level.
2. To keep meaningful dialogue occurring between the various Apostolic officials, trying to reconcile differences.
3. To initiate a more rigid but uniform standard for the ordination of clergy. (Too much latitude exists at present. The only uniform standard at present is that all say that they have been called. There needs to be inspiration and preparation for the clergy to be more effective.)
4. To help raise the standards for the selection of bishops and make them more uniform.
5. To develop a fully accredited seminary. (All the organizations that participate would have input at all levels; planning, developing, implementing, financing, staffing.)
6. To develop plans for church growth by providing assistance to small churches, new congregations, and pioneering ministers. Guidelines (such as discouraging new works within close proximity to existing Apostolic congregations) could also be drawn up.

7. To provide an information network and directory of target areas without an Apostolic witness, especially areas where contact persons reside who have expressed a desire for a church.

8. To sponsor joint financial projects such as hospitals, insurance companies, banks, food markets, and housing developments.

Since the staff in the Liaison Office would be fulltime, financing a budget has to be considered. If, for example, four different Apostolic organizations decided to participate in this venture, one procedure to be followed could be this: Every registered member of every local congregation of the four organizations would be taxed a designated amount. The amount would depend on salary ranges, and the cost of running the office. Equity would prevail because a two-hundred-member congregation would proportionally pay the same as a three-thousand-member congregation.

It is possible that a National Apostolic Liaison Office could counteract so many splits. Further, this office could assist the churches in becoming better organized.

Apostolics Have Good Points

There is positive value in the experience of speaking in tongues. Before a person experiences speaking in tongues, tremendous sacrifice has to be made in terms of opening-up to 'God. When the believer is totally open to God, he is most capable to do God's will fully, brilliantly and completely. Some may question glossolalia as a normative experience, but they certainly cannot question fruitful productivity such as occurs with a life-style of openness before God. This openness and productivity are a vital part of what Christianity is all about. Baptism in the name of Jesus Christ is the correct formula for administration. The New Testament scriptures and first century Christian church do not support the trinitarian formula. Nor do they support the idea of a Trinity.

As Apostolics we must learn to look for evidences of God-at-work among other seekers of truth. We must also learn to respect our own limitations, remembering that God is the only one who knows all. Above all, we must avoid a self-righteous attitude which boasts that:

- We are the chosen few, and the rest of you are damned.

- We don't want to go to hell, and we don't want heaven crammed.

- While our emphasis on speaking in tongues, baptism in Jesus' name, and living a holy life, are all sensible doctrines, Apostolics must begin to move toward unity rather than continued disunity, so our impact will not be less than it should

BIBLIOGRAPHY
Books

*Anderson, Arthur M., ed., *For the Defense of the Gospel.* The Writings of Bishop R. C. Lawson. New York: Church of Christ Pub. Co., 1972.

Bach, Marcus. *The Inner Ecstasy.* Nashville, TN. Abingdon Press, 1969.

Bloch-Hoell, Nils. *The Pentecostal Movement.* Oslo: Universitets Forlaget, 1964.

*Bonner, William L. *My Father in the Gospel.* New York: Greater Refuge Temple Church, s.d.

* _____ *The Uncontrolled Emotions of Saved Young People.* New York: Greater Refuge Temple Church, 1977.

* _____ *The Apostolic Dilemma, Women's Liberation. Vol. 2.,* New York: Greater Refuge Temple Church, 1976

Brumback, Carl. *What Meaneth This?* Springfield, Mo.: Gospel Pub. House, 1947.

Brunner, Frederick D. *A Theology of the Holy Spirit.* Grand Rapids, Michigan: William Eerdmans Publisher, 1970.

Burtner, Robert W. and Chiles, Robert E. (Eds.). *A Compend of Wesley's Theology.* Nashville: Abingdon Press, 1954.

Cannon. William R. *The Theology of John Wesley.* New York: Abingdon-Cokesbury Press, 1946.

Cullman. Oscar. *Baptism In The New Testament.* Chicago: Alec R. Allenson, Inc., 1950.

Damboriena, Prudencio. *Tongues As of Fire.* Washington: Corpus Books, 1969.

Fauss, Oliver F. *Baptism In God's Plan.* St. Louis, Mo.: Pentecostal Pub. House, 1955.

Funk and Wagnali's Encyclopedia, Vols, 6, 16, 19, 25.

Gilmore, Alec, ed., *Christian Baptism.* Chicago: The Judson Press, 1959.

*Golder, Morris E. *History of the Pentecostal Assemblies of the World.* Indianapolis, IN: 1973.

_____. *The Principles of Our Doctrine: What We Believe.* Indianapolis: (Indianapolis, Ind.: Grace Apostolic Church). Indianapolis, s.d.

_____*The Life and Works of Bishop Garfield Thomas Haywood.* Indianapolis: s.n., 1977.

*Haywood, Garfield T. *Before the Foundation of the World.* Indianapolis, IN: Christ Temple, 1923.

_____*The Victims of the Flaming Sword.* Indianapolis: Christ Temple Book Store, s.d.

_____*The Finest of the Wheat.* Indianapolis: Christ Temple Book Store, s.d.

_____ *The Marriage and Divorce Question in Church.* Indianapolis: Christ Temple Book Store, s.d.

_____*Ezekiel's Vision : the first chapter of Ezekiel.* Indianapolis: Christ Temple Book Store, s.d.

_____*Divine Names and Titles of Jehovah.* Indianapolis: Christ Temple Book Store, s.d.

_____*The Resurrection of the Dead.* Indianapolis: Christ Temple Book Store, s.d.

Hoekema, Anthony A. *What About Tongue-Speaking?* Grand Rapids: William E. Eerdmans Pub. Co., 1966.

Hollenweger, Walter J. *The Pentecostals.* Minneapolis, Minn.: Augsburg Pub. House, 1969.

Interpreter's Bible. Vols. 9 & 10.

Kildahl, John P. *The Psychology of Speaking in Tongues.* New York: Harper and Row, 1972.

Lindstrom, Harold. *Wesley and Sanctification.* London: Epworth Press, 1950.

Macquarrie, John. *Principles of Christian Theology*. New York: Charles Scribner's Sons, 1966.

Mills, Watson E. *Understanding Speaking in Tongues*. Grand Rapids: William B. Eerdmans Pub. Co., 1972.

Nichol, John T. *Pentecostalism*. New York: Harper and Row, Publishers, 1966.

Paterson, John. *The Real Truth About Baptism In Jesus's Name*. St. Louis, Mo.: Pentecostal Pub. House, 1953.

Ranaghan, Kevin and Dorothy. *Catholic Pentecostals*. New York: Paulist Press Deus Books, 1969.

Richardson, Alan, ed., *A Dictionary of Christian Theology*. Philadelphia: Westminster Press, 1969.

*Richardson, James C. *Believer's Guide Books*. Martinsville, Virginia: 1973.

Samarian, William J. *Tongues of Men and Angels*. New York: Macmillan Co., 1972.

Schlink, Edmund. *The Doctrine of Baptism*. St. Louis: Concordia Pub. House, 1972.

Schmidt, Martin. *John Wesley, A Theological Biography*. New York: Abingdon Press, 1962.

Synan, Vinson. *The Holiness-Pentecostal Movement in the United States*. Grand Rapids: William B. Eerdmans Pub. Co., 1971.

*Thompson, Jr., Walter , ed., *50th Anniversary Jubilee, The Way of the Cross Church of Christ, Inc.* Washington, DC: 1978.

*Wheeler, Carrie, ed., *The Path of Life Through Highway Christian Church of Christ, s.l.: s.n., 1968*.

Williams, Colin W. *John Wesley's Theology Today*. New York: Abingdon Press, 1960.

*Williams, Evelyn M., ed., *Sermons and Teachings of Bishop H. C. Brooks*. Washington, DC: s.n., 1964.

*Williams, Smallwood E. *Significant Sermons*. Washington, DC: Bible Way Church Press, 1970.

Articles

Forbes, Jr., James A., "A Ministry of Hope from a Double Ministry," *Theological Education,* Vol. 9, No. 4, Supplement, 1973.

Tinney, James S., "Black Origins of the Pentecostal Movement," *Christianity Today,* Vol. 16, No. 1, 1971.

Minutes and Disciplines

*Bowers, Paul A., ed., 1972 *Minute Book of the Pentecostal Assemblies of the World.* Indianapolis, Inc.

* 1976 *Minute Book of the Pentecostal Assemblies of the World.* Indianapolis, Inc.

*Davis, Samuel B., ed., 1972 *Minute and Church Directory of The Way of the Cross Church of Christ.* Washington, D. C.

* 1975 *Minutes and Church Directory of The Way of the Cross Church of Christ.* Hartford, Conn.: Brooks Chapel Press, 1976.

* 1978 *Minutes and Church Directory of The Way of the Cross Church of Christ.* Hartford, Conn.: Brooks Chapel Press, 1979.

*Johnson, Loretta and Prescott, Arbadella (Eds.). 1972 *Minutes of the Apostle Church of Christ in God.* Martinsville, Virginia.

*Lawson, Robert C. *Discipline Book of the Church of Our Lord Jesus Christ.* New York, 1968.

*Neal, Eli N. and Smith, D. E., eds. *Discipline of The Church of God (Apostolic)*

*Richardson, James C., ed., *Discipline, Apostle Church of Christ In God.* Martinsville, Virginia.

* _____. *Discipline Book of the Apostle Church of Christ In God.* Martinsville, Virginia.

*Robinson, R. L., ed., 1952 *Minute Book of the Pentecostal Assemblies of The World.* Indianapolis.

*Saunders, Monroe R. *Church Order and Discipline of the United Church of Jesus Christ Apostolic.* Washington, D.C., 1965.

*Williams, Smallwood E. *Rules and Regulations of the Bible Way Church of Our Lord Jesus Christ World Wide.* Washington, D.C.: Bible Way Church Press, 1962.

*Woolfork, T. E., ed., 1977 *Minute Book, Church of Our Lord Jesus Christ, Fifty-Eighth Session.* New York, N.Y.: Greater Refuge Temple.

Primary materials written by Black Apostolics.

Made in the USA
Middletown, DE
02 June 2023

31925267R00118